Praise for *Tackle What's Next*

"If anyone is qualified to help you determine your 'What's Next' it's Eric Wood. I have witnessed his preparation and process firsthand. It has worked for him, and it will work for you. His real-life experiences represent powerful, inspiring examples of walking the talk."

—David Novak,
Cofounder and Former CEO of YUM! Brands Inc.;
Founder and CEO of Novak Leadership

"Eric Wood has excelled at every major transition in his life. He has a unique ability to see the future and execute on the present. I've personally been so impressed with the levels of wisdom and discernment Eric demonstrates in navigating transition. He's thoughtful, prayerful, and deliberate. Eric is a first-class example of what it means to lead through change and find success in every chapter of life!"

—Jordan Montgomery,
Speaker and Performance Coach

"As a football player, content creator, business leader, and family man, Eric Wood is a man whose ambition I admire and respect. He relentlessly strives for growth and improvement. Ambition propels him forward, but humility and wisdom keep his course steady. This book offers insight that enables its readers to step boldly into whatever is next with a healthy blend of ambition, humility, and wisdom."

—Kyle Idleman,
Head Pastor, Southeast Christian Church, and Bestselling Author

"Eric has always been someone I look up to. As his teammate with the Buffalo Bills, I watched him apply the principles discussed in his new book daily. When he was faced with adversity at the end of his career, he chose to continue growing and learning. In this book, there are priceless lessons on how to overcome adversity and attack life daily on your terms. This is a powerful book that will push you to become better day by day."

—Richie Incognito,
Four-time NFL Pro Bowl Guard, 16-year NFL veteran

"There are knowers and there are learners. A knower has stopped learning and thinks they know it all, but a learner remains hungry and teachable. The latter describes Eric Wood. Fortunately, in *Tackle What's Next* you have the opportunity to glean from his leadership learnings the very same lessons that have allowed him to successfully transition through the seasons of life."

—Dave Stone,
Former Pastor, Southeast Christian Church

"Oftentimes, folks wonder what it is like to be a professional athlete. Everyone sees what happens on game day, but rarely does the day-to-day come to light, especially when the playing days come to an end. Not only does Eric Wood share his personal story of how things ended but also he has found a way for his readers to apply the coping mechanisms and strategies he developed to fulfill their own 'What's Next.' Eric's post-NFL career success comes as no surprise to me, and seeing how he has achieved this success can help many people apply his story to their own situations."

—Kyle Rudolph,
Two-time NFL Pro Bowl Tight End

TACKLE WHAT'S NEXT

FOREWORD BY **SEAN MCDERMOTT**
HEAD COACH OF THE NFL BUFFALO BILLS

ERIC WOOD
NFL PRO BOWL VETERAN

TACKLE WHAT'S NEXT

OWN YOUR STORY

STACK WINS

ACHIEVE YOUR GOALS
IN **BUSINESS** AND **LIFE**

WILEY

Library of Congress Cataloging-in-Publication Data:
Names: Wood, Eric, 1986- author.
Title: Tackle what's next : own your story, stack wins, and achieve your goals in business and life / by Eric Wood.
Description: Hoboken, New Jersey : Wiley, [2023] | Includes index. | Description based on print version record and CIP data provided by publisher; resource not viewed.
Identifiers: LCCN 2022020191 (print) | LCCN 2022020192 (ebook) | ISBN 9781119931881 (epub) | ISBN 9781119931874 (adobe pdf) | ISBN 9781119931867 (cloth) | ISBN 9781119931867 (cloth) | ISBN 9781119931874 (adobe pdf) | ISBN 9781119931881 (epub)
Subjects: LCSH: Self-actualization (Psychology)
Classification: LCC BF637.S4 (ebook) | LCC BF637.S4 W6577 2023 (print) | DDC 158.1 23/eng/20220—dc17
LC record available at https://lccn.loc.gov/2022020191
LC ebook record available at https://lccn.loc.gov/2022020192

Cover Design: Paul McCarthy

SKY10035792_081922

To my wife, Leslie, and two kids, Grace and Garrett,
for whom I strive to be a better man every day.

CONTENTS

FOREWORD

Sean McDermott

When Eric told me he was writing a book about how to move on from big moments of transition, I knew he was the right man for the job.

I first met him in 2017 after joining the Bills, and his reputation preceded him. The strength coach at the Carolina Panthers was a big fan of Eric and had worked with him at Louisville. He told me an impressive story about Eric lunging toward the finish line just so he could finish first in an off-season conditioning drill. He was just known as the guy who was always giving an all-out effort.

And that's exactly what I saw when we began working together in Buffalo. Here was this outstanding and talented player who backed it up with preparation and work. Because of his approach to the game, I felt we were somewhat equally aligned early on in our time together. We had a similar approach and I knew that this was a player who would help get us off the ground and help get us there to where we are today.

The word *process* gets thrown out a lot in football, but that's because it's still the foundation of excellent performance. If you study peak performers in any industry, in particular sports, once they have a great process down, the day-by-day routine, which basically in our business is Monday through Saturday, or the entire off-season, it sure makes things a lot easier come September through February.

Those who stick to their process consistently give themselves the best chance to be peak performers in their line of work.

Eric takes that process with a standard, that daily set of consistent actions, and applies it to every facet of his life.

Off the field, he is a dedicated family man, a man of deep faith, and someone who committed a significant portion of his life and energy to charity and serving others.

In 2017, Eric was on the team that helped break our 17-year drought. Unfortunately, his momentum was cut short because he was forced to retire early from football because of a physical issue. Yet he took that same approach of process and preparation to get him through the next big thing off the field.

Retiring early can be rough on many players, yet he's done a remarkable job taking the next steps and applying that faithful day-to-day process to the other parts of his life. I'm extremely proud of him and admire him for that. It's not easy to do.

I always thought Eric had a way of drawing people to him, no matter what he was doing. He's a connector of people off the field and on the field. One weekend he's at the Kentucky Derby, and the next, he's announcing a game. He does college football games in the fall, and then he gives back to Louisville, where he's an important part of the community. And then, before you know it, he's announcing a Bills game up on a Sunday. Did I mention he has a wife and kids, too? Put all those jobs together—how does he have time for that? Amazing!

He has a lot on his shoulders, but it always seems like he balances it extremely well, which speaks to his days as a player. He's able to balance things and all these disparate interests in life, which allows him to be a great leader.

I know there are many people who struggle with major transitions in life. Take a page from Eric's playbook—take a close look at your process and what you're doing every day.

I know you'll be inspired by Eric's journey and adopt those basic principles that will lead to great success on your own path.

PREFACE

You're Right Where You Need to Be Right Now

The best day of your life is the one on which you decide your life is your own. No apologies or excuses. No one to rely on or blame. The gift is yours, it's an amazing journey, and you alone are responsible for the quality of it.

—Bob Moawad

Now is the perfect time to get prepared for what's next.

Whether you are riding on top of the world, or having a rough time of it, or somewhere in between, you are perfectly positioned to make your "what's next" your best yet. No matter how comfortable or uncomfortable you are, or what the circumstances of your life might be, no matter where you are in the world or what you have done or not done, this is the perfect time to get prepared.

If you're going through a rough transition in life right now, what if this is the perfect packaged discomfort to prod you to make a shift in your life to make things better? What if all this pain is fertilizer for your growth? What if all this confusion is just what the doctor ordered to get you to your next step? And what if I show you some tools that helped me get to my what's next when I was going through a rough transition myself?

What if there was nothing wrong with you at all and that these "bad circumstances" are fuel to make you more extraordinary?

Conversely, what if you're feeling pretty on top of your game and cruising through life right now? Maybe you're a sports fan or a big Bills fan, and you happened to pick up this book. What if implementing the principles in this book can make your life even better, get you to places you only imagined, and help you achieve success in all of the buckets of your life?

What if you're only scratching the surface of what's possible for you?

Either way, this book is for you. If this book is in your hands, you were meant to pick it up for a reason. You're right where you need to be right now, even though it may not make sense. I wrote this book to give you some proven tools to help prepare you for the next, best chapter of your life. I believe God has great things in store for all of you.

In 2017, when I started the football season, I was out to have my best season yet with the Buffalo Bills—and we did! At that point, I wasn't looking to make a change either. Yet life took an unexpected direction, and I was forced to change. I had to completely alter my perspective and take stock of what "winning" would look like from here on out and what it would take.

The truth is, everyone can prepare to win in any endeavor, but not everyone does. To quote Jerry Rice, "Today I will do what others won't, so tomorrow I will do what others can't."

Your day is today, and by following the principles of this book, your what's next will be your best yet.

1 The Pivot Point

"For I know the plans I have for you," declares the Lord, "plans to prosper you and not to harm you, plans to give you hope and a future."
—Jeremiah 29:11

Let me tell you about the most extraordinary football season of my life, a time where I felt that God was smiling on me and the sky was the limit in my career. It's strange thinking about that time now because what I didn't know then was that it would all be over in an instant.

First of all, I love professional football. I love everything about it. I love the competitiveness (I'm the most competitive person I know!), the camaraderie, the teamwork, the discipline, the preparation, the intensity, and the physicality of it. For me, it was part of the American dream, to pursue something and be passionate about it, to be successful at something, and go try to be the very best you can be. Along with that, it was just so much fun and brought so much abundance to my family and me. To play football as a profession has been one of the biggest blessings of my life.

In 2009, I was a first-round draft pick by the Buffalo Bills. I played my entire nine-year career with the Bills, and they offered me an extended contract twice before my ninth season in the NFL. In my final year on my second deal with the Bills, I contemplated what I wanted to do next. Should I stick around, or should I maybe hit free agency? The Bills had been really good to me, and I loved all those guys. They were some of the best of the best. Yet there was always the temptation to try something new, to challenge myself differently.

What made the decision easy for me was that the Bills just hired Sean McDermott and Brandon Beane, and I truly trusted their vision for the organization. I also couldn't imagine the Bills breaking the longest playoff drought in the NFL and me not be a part of it. I had put so much blood, sweat, and tears into playing for the Bills, and I needed to be there for when the tide turned and the Bills would be successful again. With my faith in the Bills secure, I signed a contract extension before my ninth season—the very special 2017 season.

You see, the Buffalo Bills hadn't made it to the playoffs for 17 years. And we were going to be the winning team configuration to break that drought. That didn't seem like the way it would be at first. We traded away our most recent top picks that the previous regime had drafted, and many outsiders thought we were tanking. Tanking is when a team will intentionally have a bad season in order to get better draft picks and try to set the organization up for long-term success.

Tanking is a nightmare for veterans on a team. Would I even be around by the time this team would be good enough to make the playoffs? Would I be cut or traded to ensure a losing season? Did I really want to take on the physicality of an NFL season when we have no shot at making the playoffs?

Our leadership council met with Sean McDermott, and he was explaining that we were, in fact, not tanking. We were simply trying to build a team of players that had a certain type of DNA that would set the culture for long-term success, and Sean felt that this could also lead to success in the short term as well. Although it didn't make full sense to all of us in that meeting, we put our trust in the Bills' front office that we were going to go out and be in a "win-now" mode.

It turned out to be the perfect strategy, along with the exact right combination of players and leadership. After we had won our final game of the season against the Dolphins, we watched from the locker room as the Bengals beat the Ravens to send us to the playoffs. Professionally, that was one of the most joyful moments of my life. (If you're curious, you can go on YouTube and watch our celebration.)

Life was good. I already had my contract in place. My beautiful wife, Leslie, was in the late stages of pregnancy, about ready to pop with our second child. I figured that she, the kids, and I would be in Buffalo through year 11 at that point. We had a house up there, and we lived back and forth between Buffalo, New York, and Louisville, Kentucky. I felt unbelievably lucky to have so many blessings and positive things in my life all at once.

Because my second child was so close to being born, I had an unusual attitude heading into the Jacksonville game. We were either going to beat Jacksonville and move on into the second round of the playoffs, or we would lose the game, and I would get to witness the birth of my son. It was a win-win situation for me, something I wasn't used to feeling about possibly losing a big game. As I said, I'm very competitive.

Our game was scheduled for a Sunday, and Leslie was being induced on Wednesday. We ended up losing in Jacksonville, 10–3. All players must get an exit physical the day after the last game of the season. So we lost on Sunday, and the team doctor wanted me to do an exit physical on Monday morning.

So the season ends. I'm the only player on the team that played 100% of the snaps that year—which is pretty rare in the NFL because you could either be beating a team really badly, and they pull the starters, or you could be losing by a ton, and they could pull the starters (both had happened to me in previous years of my career). Also, injuries pop up all of the time when you would have to miss snaps, or your shoe could even come untied to cause you to miss a play. I was an alternate for the Pro Bowl, and there were two centers in the playoffs. So the chances of me going to the Pro Bowl were pretty good.

I was in a hurry to get out of Buffalo to go catch the birth of my son, but the doctor insisted I get an MRI before I leave town.

And I said, "Look, I'm good. I'm the only player who played all the snaps. Please send me home. I'm going to get out of here because I'm going to go catch the birth of my son."

"Well, you had these stingers this year," he said. "Just go out and get an MRI on your neck."

I didn't want to hear it. If you're unfamiliar with "stingers," they're a common ailment suffered by football players in particular. It's a tingling feeling in the hand or arm resulting from a nerve injury in the neck or shoulder. If you've ever played high school football, chances are you or someone on your team had a stinger at least once. And that's precisely what I told the doctor! "My buddies in high school had stingers! Why do I need to get an MRI for a stinger?" The whole situation seemed ridiculous.

But he said, "You know, it's kind of alarming that you never suffered a stinger until this season." So I gave in and got an MRI, hopped into my car, and drove back to Louisville as fast as I could to be with my wife for the birth of our son. I wouldn't get the MRI results right away, but I wasn't anxious about it.

Honestly, that MRI was the furthest thing from my mind on that Wednesday. There I was, in the hospital waiting room, about 50 minutes from my son being born, and I get the call.

It was the call that ended my career.

The MRI revealed that in my cervical column, at points C2 and C3, I had disc and bone penetrating into my spinal cord. The doctors were not sure why or how I wasn't lying motionless on a football field, but that's what the MRI indicated should have happened to cause this. They told me this injury meant I could no longer play football. I thought, *How could this be?*

At first, I was in complete denial. I brought up that Peyton Manning had a neck fusion; why couldn't I? I found myself thinking there must be some way out, like, is there any way we can make this surgery work?

I found out later that Manning's neck fusion was lower in his spine. Everything is less stable toward the top, and when you hurt your spinal cord, it affects everything below it. C2 and C3 are too high on the spinal column to do the same kind of fusion procedure.

The doctors told me I was lucky I wasn't more affected by the injury than I was with only the stingers. They told me I was fortunate just to have walked away from the field. They also said that even though there was a chance at a successful surgery, I would never pass a football physical again.

So this situation was serious. The doctors stressed that if I got hit the wrong way with this kind of injury, I could be a paraplegic and lose my ability to breathe on my own without machines. And that hit me close to home.

You see, my little brother, Evan, was born with severe cerebral palsy. He never walked, talked, or breathed on his own. I saw firsthand what that looked like. He fought and lived for 11 years—and it was hard to watch him struggle. I was 14 when he passed. And so to get that news and be able to picture myself in my brother and what could have happened—well, that was a little intense for me.

I was at the crossroads of "grateful it's not worse" but also devastated that I had to face this. I got the news that my career was over, and it just shocked me. I know that it happens to a lot of guys, but, honestly, at that moment, I just felt cheated because I felt like I had put in so much work to that point.

I mean, I had so much joy on a day-to-day basis in that facility. I was a captain for three years, and it should have been five. Rex Ryan, the head coach of the Buffalo Bills, doesn't do captains. He does game captains. So instead of having the gold patch on my jersey signifying five-plus years of being captain with the same team, I only had three stars filled in. That's okay, though. I loved playing for Rex Ryan. Honestly, I loved everything about playing professional football.

I did love my role. I loved the platform it gave me, too. I was using my platform to bring people into my men's group at church during the off-season. I was bringing people closer to their faith, closer to God.

I was playing with a lot of freedom as well. Just knowing that "hey, I can give it all I've got, and I don't have to be ashamed." And I wanted that Super Bowl. I was so looking forward to making playoff runs. I was also going to miss Buffalo terribly, a great city that had welcomed me with open arms and I had come to know and love.

I loved it all, and at that moment, I was totally crushed.

It was such a rollercoaster of emotions because my son was about to born. I told my wife the news, and she started to cry. A nurse came in and said to her, "Honey, honey, it's not going to hurt that bad." And she said, "It's not about the baby!" We laughed about that later, but at the time, it was far from funny for anyone in the room.

My son was born 50 minutes later, and it was such an immense rush of joy, such a distraction from the previous moment. It was a tremendous gift he came when he did because I think his arrival at that moment helped me process what was happening in the big picture. I had this incredible blessing of a son. However, I also had one of the top neurological doctors in the country telling me I would never play football again (later, I would get eight more second opinions from neurologists—they all agreed). It was one significant scary change accompanied by a huge joyful change.

So for me, I hit that **pivot point.** I'll explain what I mean.

For the Buffalo Bills, I played the center position, often known as the "pivot" because of its central location on the field. The center is in the middle of the offensive formation. Because he starts the play with the ball, the offense's formation is dictated by where the center lines up. Some may say it's the most pivotal position on the field because, without a clean snap to the quarterback, the play has no chance for success. (Or maybe that's just how a former center sees it.)

In that sense, the word *pivot* is being used as a noun. It is the central place on the field. The pivot of a city is often the metropolitan area around which all the rest of the city revolves. The pivot of a house is usually the kitchen, from which all other rooms of the house flow. The pivot of an organization would be the leader, from which all decisions are made or passed through.

Then there's the pivot that requires action. I've had my share of experiences in this brand of pivoting, both on and off the football field. But this was the most significant pivot of my life, ending my ability to play football forever. I was forced to pivot in my entire career and from a lifestyle that I was very accustomed to living.

It wasn't like I hit rock bottom at that moment. It took a while. It took some days of anxiety trying to figure out what I was all about moving forward and how I would proceed. All my eggs were in one basket, career-wise. My whole life was football, and I was absolutely all in. I didn't have a next career lined up by any means. But when you hit that pivot point, there are some action steps that you need to take personally.

Along with that came a lot of personal development work and consciously working on my inner game and how I look at and function in life. Those steps didn't come all at once for me. Looking back, it wasn't like I got out of the league, and suddenly I had an epiphany or this blueprint of what to do. I got a lot of good advice from incredible people, and I've seen and practiced what works firsthand.

One thing that worked in my favor is the way I'm wired. I'm always thinking, "What's next? How can I make my future bigger than my past?" I just know that whatever is happening was happening for a reason.

I also had tremendous faith that God had something planned for me. Like he could help me take this traumatic event in my life and show me something exceptional that I could do with it. I just wasn't sure what that was yet. But I knew that he had plans for me and would help me prosper. I knew that I had hope and a future and that he could help me make this into a blessing.

Now, I got a lot of help in the aftermath of my forced retirement. I hit a point of obscurity for the first time in a long time because the Bills hadn't officially released me, so I couldn't go out and get a job. National media members had reached out, and I appreciate all of their help in my transition. They wanted to help me get into the sports broadcast business. But I couldn't even accept a job until June because of my contract with the Bills. By that time, all of the broadcast crews were filled for the upcoming season.

Sports broadcasting is a natural transition for many athletes who retire—they want to get into the media world, because for most of us, that's all we have known for a significant part of our lives. But you have to do it right away because if you wait a few years and you're an offensive lineman who played in western New York, they're going to say, "Who are you again?" And so I wanted to give it a shot, but I couldn't even go out and try and get a job. It wasn't like *Monday Night Football* came calling, but the help from so many individuals led me to be a color analyst for the Buffalo Bills Radio broadcast as well as an analyst for ESPN/ACC network.

I've also been fortunate because I've been able to create a new platform through my podcast, "What's Next with Eric Wood." In the beginning, I looked at it as a medium to interview other athletes and talk about football and my time with the Bills. But as time went on, the scope became so much more vast. I found myself interviewing people who had fantastic advice to offer on how to lead a more effective and impactful life, people who had all faced a pivot point moment of their own and made it work for them. Spending time with all those people began to shift my thinking and change my life for the better as well.

Our new tagline became "Interviews That Impact and Inspire." My podcast guests were changing lives, including mine, and I could use my platform to amplify their message. I find such joy in serving and uplifting others, and my show has become a vital part of that for me. I may never have connected with so many inspirational and transformative people had my life gone exactly the way I expected.

On top of all this, amid my transition, barely two years retired from the NFL, the COVID-19 pandemic hit. Suddenly, millions of others were experiencing a dramatic pivot point themselves in the aftermath. Many of them did not have the tools they need to process it or know exactly how they were going to pivot. So many felt like they'd had the rug pulled out from under them. And the ancillary effects of this pandemic are going to be felt for years down the line. Countless people are hanging on by a thread financially, or worse, have lost loved ones. Or both. How do you pivot from those moments? That's part of why I decided I needed to write this book now.

The principles I write about are incredibly useful in practically any situation where you find yourself in the middle of a big transition. It doesn't have to be a global pandemic or a disaster. It could be anything from moving to a new place, or getting married for the first time, starting a new career, becoming a parent, dealing with a loss, or any variety of crossroads. Maybe you just want to be more effective at what you are already doing or bring more abundance into your life.

Think of each chapter as a different play in a playbook, the top strategies I've found so far for getting you to your personal what's next. The principles, or "plays," work best when done in combination with all the others. I can't take credit for all the ideas—so many of these words of wisdom have been passed down through the generations in multiple forms.

I always believed in taking advice from those further along on their journey in life. In football, one of the most valuable things to do when you enter the NFL is to find a veteran on the team and emulate his daily habits and routines. As I transitioned into my next chapter, those referenced in this book taught me and will teach you so many valuable lessons that you can implement to enhance your life.

I'm putting my particular spin on it in a way that I hope you'll find accessible. One of my greatest gifts that I'm learning to own is my ability to connect with others, and I want you to feel that you're getting practical support from me in a way that can help you get the things you want in your life. I genuinely do want to serve you and uplift you to more extraordinary things!

Unlike an actual football playbook, there are not nearly as many plays to remember. Once you start using them, they will become second nature. However, similar to an actual playbook, all the plays require diligent practice. All the concepts are not complicated, but you must act on them to get any benefit. Just like out on the field, you will naturally be better at some plays than others, so don't be discouraged if a few take time to become habits.

I've learned so much over the past few years from my journey and my incredible podcast guests. When I'm sharing a little nugget of wisdom from them, I'll be sure to point out who said it so you can dig deeper into their way of thinking as well. Once you go down the rabbit hole of inspiration, you may notice a positive ripple effect on your life sooner than you expect.

I believe God has a plan for us, and part of my plan is to help others step into their greatness. When you transform yourself, you improve the lives of everyone around you. Your what's next may inspire and change those closest to you in ways that you can't imagine.

Whatever is going on in your life, just remember your future is so much bigger than your past!

Let me serve you, and help you embrace it!

2 Examine Your Gifts

Your talent is God's gift to you. What you do with it is your gift back to God.

—Leo Buscaglia

When you find yourself down, disappointed that you've arrived at a place you never thought you'd be, it's easy to live in despair. Taking a look around, it can seem like everything is against you, and your luck has run out. My first instinct is to reach out to you and suggest that you're not starting from zero. Wherever you are in your life, you've merely reached a transition point, where you are moving from one way of life to the next. Choose to use your adversity to propel you upward.

You're here on earth with a full slate of natural gifts that you've used all your life, gifts that will continue to serve you as you get to the next step. If you're having a hard time imagining what those gifts are, it might be because you use them instinctively without thinking about them. Something else that often happens when you find yourself down is that you have trouble seeing your attributes and resources. You have more tools in your utility belt than you give yourself credit for. Trust me; I was exactly in the same boat.

When I hit my period of transition, between when my football career had abruptly ended and I had not yet found a new direction, I was experiencing a gap. It was a period of not knowing, and after years and years of rigid physical discipline, I was uncertain of what

NOT always necessary
Just Be

exactly I was supposed to do and where I was supposed to go. Though I had faith that I would find out, I didn't yet have the answers at my fingertips. It was just a lot of big questions.

I would wake up in the morning and think, "Okay, what the heck am I going to do next?" I meant that in two ways. One was the broad figurative sense, as in, "Where am I going with my life?" But I also meant it in the day-by-day sense, as in, "What the heck am I doing after breakfast?" Sometimes it was the smaller question that was hard to answer.

When I was training in the NFL, I had accounted for almost every minute of every day. What and when I ate, how often I worked out and when, and what weight I needed to be. I was on autopilot in a good way—every single thing that I did in my daily schedule was to help me be the best I could be at professional football. From that directive, my daily schedule trickled down to what I would be doing every minute of the day.

Well, I couldn't play football anymore.

So for me, the first step after asking myself what I was going to do next meant taking football out of the equation and taking a detailed look at who I was on a deep level. To answer that question, I had to begin with examining my gifts.

As luck would have it, I had started working with an executive coach months before my pivot point and forced retirement. If you've never worked with an executive coach, a good way of looking at it is someone similar to an athletic coach, but for your business and life goals. Someone to help you make the right plays in life, go over the metaphorical game tape, and give you feedback that will help you get to where you want to go. My coach's name is James McPartland, but to his high-level clients and me, he just goes by "Mac."

A teammate of mine was getting reinstated back in the NFL. As a condition, they wanted him to work with a therapist. Mac wasn't

precisely a therapist. However, in terms of the impact he made on other people's lives, one could argue that he was an equivalent.
I served as my teammate's accountability partner and "eyes on the ground" for Mac. So, Mac and I would talk once a month for maybe 20 minutes. I was basically confirming that my teammate was doing everything on the straight and narrow (he was).

I was a bit new to this, and I liked the results I saw from my teammate regarding his overall life improvement. I was curious about this whole coaching process.

So, I started professional executive coaching six months prior to my career ending, even though I didn't know it was about to end. I was glad I was working with him beforehand to help me get into the right mindset when my big transition did come.

One of the first things Mac asked me to do was to examine what my gifts were. He started with a list of questions to help me discover them. Now, these aren't the only questions you can ask yourself to start finding your gifts, but they are great questions. The first was basic and intuitive.

Question 1: What Are You Good at Naturally?

This question was tricky because I felt one of my most significant gifts was one I wasn't allowed to use anymore: my natural athletic ability and my God-given shape and size. Now, I know some of that's developed through weight training and drills, but my little brother is 5'10" and 175 pounds. By contrast, I was gifted a body that could be an NFL center. I could be deadly on the field. If I couldn't use that body the way I've trained it, how could that translate into something else?

That was a great place to start. I've been a natural athlete for as long as I remember. I grew up in a huge neighborhood with tons of kids. I could probably ride my bike for a mile without ever running into a main road. We'd play roller hockey, basketball, whatever it was, and we got after it. Even as a kid, I wanted to win, no matter what I was playing. We developed skills and a competitive spirit that I sometimes worry my kids won't get, growing up in a smaller neighborhood without many young kids.

And there was one of my gifts right there: a competitive spirit. Even if you took away all of my athletic ability, even if I were in a wheelchair, I would still have that natural competitiveness. I always want to be the best at whatever I'm doing, which pushes me and can serve me no matter what career path I choose from here on out. If I pick up something new that I think is worthwhile, I always want to learn faster and excel.

Question 2: What Have You Learned to Do Well?

This question is my personal variation on the first question that Mac asked me. Sometimes we learn to be very good at something that started as a natural knack or talent and honed it into something special.

I've always felt I was a good communicator. But it was my training in football that took that skill from good to great. When you're a center, a lot of what you do is communicating to the other players in real time. So much happens very quickly.

Sometimes I found myself in third-and-long situations—the defense was moving, and I had to give everybody on offense blocking assignments to counteract these experienced genius defensive coordinators' plans. It's not easy, either, because sometimes you've seen the plays, or something similar, only on film, but they're actually going to run another defensive scheme in disguise, which confuses you. So, I would be trying to get everyone on the same page in about 10 seconds, and I would still have to do my job of snapping the football and then start blocking an elite defender.

As a long-tenured veteran for the Bills, I was communicating as a mouthpiece for the organization and for the players on my team. You have to be good at getting the right message across. The last thing you want to do is embarrass the team or say something that just wasn't accurate. You also want to do much more than that; you want to inspire and represent the best of what your team has to offer.

Playing in the NFL also forces you to get used to answering questions in front of a camera. Whether it is after practice or games, you must make yourself available to the media to answer questions. If you don't do this, it can result in a fine (remember Marshawn Lynch at the Super Bowl media day famously saying, "I'm only here so I don't get fined."). I would always try to be insightful for those media sessions because I understood that even if I wasn't in the mood for it that day, those media members have a job to do and should be treated with respect, especially because most were always so supportive of and respectful to me.

Those times in front of a camera were sharpening my craft of communication, even if I didn't recognize it as such at the moment.

To build on my gifts, I chose to start by getting into sports broadcasting and producing my own podcast. I could leverage my communication skills to adapt to those mediums quickly, and each of those paths had so many more gifts and resources to offer me down the road. There was still a tremendous learning curve—learning the art of a conversation for a podcast interview is very different from doing a radio interview or a sideline interview. They are all related but still distinct skills. Each of the various disciplines took practice and dedicated learning, like any other skill.

Question 3: What Do People Who Love You Say Your Gifts Are?

Mac made a point of asking me this question.

Sometimes your gifts are obvious to everyone but yourself. The people who love you and know you the best are keenly aware of your qualities and attributes, and your life partner can sometimes shine a light on any areas that you may not be clear on. Somehow, it's easier to get it when someone else can see it in you. It seems like proof or confirmation.

My wife, Leslie, and I were doing a couple's Bible study with Dave and Beth Stone, whom you can hear from on my podcast. We were at their house, and we were doing an exercise in which we were looking at spiritual gifts. As part of the exercise, we had to write down what all those gifts were that we saw in our partner. I thought maybe Leslie would write down *joy* or *faithfulness*. But she surprised me. She wrote *self-discipline*. That didn't seem like an awe-inspiring "gift" at first.

Then I started thinking about it and realized that self-discipline had served me well my whole life and was primarily responsible for my football career, even more so than my natural athletic ability.

Self-discipline is a commitment—a daily sacrifice, steps that you do every single day. It's not a one-time thing. When I was a junior in high school, I wasn't first string on our varsity football team. I was a backup tight end and hadn't made the switch to the offensive line yet, where I would excel later. I considered myself more of a basketball player at the time. We had this "Practice Player of the Day" jersey, and whoever practiced the hardest and had the best practice overall would get to wear that jersey the next practice.

In basketball, I was probably a hard worker, but I wasn't *that* hard of a worker. At that point, you never would have looked around the high school and said, "Eric Wood is the hardest worker we have." But things were about to change.

Now, my senior year, I wanted that "Practice Player of the Day" jersey every single day. And I committed to it. I wanted it at a gut level because when the college coaches came around to recruit people for basketball or football, I'd have a different color jersey throughout that entire basketball season. I kept it the whole year! After every practice, we voted on who got the "Practice Player the Day" jersey, and it wasn't purely the points (or else I may have never got it). A lot of it was the effort, and I kept at the entire season because I said, "I can't let someone else have this on if Louisville shows up tomorrow, or if the University of Cincinnati, or whoever it may be, walks in the door. I've got to have it on."

Well, after months and months of pushing yourself to the limit, you become accustomed to that level of practice. You become conditioned to that, and then it became uncomfortable for me not to be the hardest worker. That began a lifetime of doubling down and trying to outwork everyone else on the field to excel. (There's that competitive spirit again.) While at Louisville, I would win the award for the hardest worker in the off-season, and I would win it again playing in the NFL for the Bills. You can't control everything in sports, but you can control your effort and your discipline.

I wasn't a starter on varsity football until my senior year in high school—that year, I played both basketball and football. I got some good advice to put on some weight to play on the offensive line and move from the tight end position. So, I put on 55 pounds. I didn't play basketball my junior year of high school to put on weight for football. I feel at times in our lives we have to give up "good things" for "great things," even if we love them. I wouldn't have been able to put on the weight for football if I had played basketball my junior year, and that made an enormous impact on my life, despite the fact that I truly missed playing basketball that year.

That self-discipline kept serving me. When I went to the University of Louisville, I set our strength and conditioning record with "Big House" Joe Kenn; he was the only strength coach ever to be the national strength coach of the year in the NFL and college. I broke his all-time conditioning record at 300 pounds.

My little brother Evan never got to walk. So how was I ever going to complain about running? I would take that mindset to it.

So, I'm going to give it my all. I'm never going to be late. I'm always going to be prepared. I am going to show up ready to roll. If you come in with that mentality every day, you get results over the weeks and years. That part of you almost goes on autopilot. I'm going to cover more about how to stack good habits in Chapter 7.

It's incredible what happened five years later. I redshirted my first year at Louisville. I spent four and a half years there and then ended up a first-round draft pick for the Buffalo Bills. I received some excellent advice when I got there. Someone said, "Watch the undrafted free agents work. They better never outwork you if you want to be the best. You have to outwork every undrafted free agent, and then you can put that first-round draft pick title beside you." I took that to heart and followed his advice.

It's wonderful what conscious, consistent effort through self-discipline can bring.

Question 4: What Are You Resisting?

Mac likes this question in particular because it can unearth some things that are just under the surface. When we resist certain things, it can be a clue where our head is, and that can tell us where we need to go. Sometimes what we resist is a gift we have to offer the world.

At the beginning of my forced retirement, I like to think I took the right attitude. I didn't feel like I was resisting anything. I felt like I was doing the opposite—just totally accepting and trusting that God had a plan for me. I knew God would give me hope and a future and that my next thing would be my best thing.

The only catch was I thought it would happen a lot sooner. I was still without a clear next thing on my plate just yet. Suddenly, I had questions about what my purpose was and what my daily purpose would look like. Well, now I was trying to be the best . . . at what, exactly? Spiritually, I knew I had a solid foundation. I just didn't know where or what I was going to build.

I wish I had a better name for what happened to me next. I call it "Who gives a crap" mode for lack of a better phrase. For the first time in my life, it didn't really matter. If I wasn't a center anymore, what's the worst that could happen if I didn't work out? If I had a healthy meal, it really didn't matter. If I sat on the couch and watched TV, it didn't really matter. None of those would hurt my football performance because there was no more football.

So, I kept thinking, "who gives a crap?" There's no one measuring this. Sure, there were metrics, but it just didn't really matter. And I say this from a humble place—the game of football blessed me with a financial circumstance that most of the work I was doing didn't affect our lifestyle that much. We didn't spend a ton of money while I was playing. We live in Louisville, Kentucky. We could maintain this lifestyle whether I went out and compete super hard at business or not.

It was less depression and more anxiety, because I think, deep down, I'm always striving to beat that yesterday version of myself. I'm rarely down in the dumps. But this time I was down. For the first time in my life, I didn't have structure and order. I didn't have accountability, built-in goal orientation, or a built-in community. I had no apparent tribe.

"Who gives a crap" mode is a hazardous spot. I talked about this recently on a podcast, and it seems to have struck a chord. I had four former NFL guys reach out to me immediately on Instagram and said, "Dude, you hit that right on the money." I think that we all feel like we had our identities ripped out.

What I eventually came to realize is that it's not about me. I finally snapped out of it and realized that God had given me gifts to *serve and encourage others*. He has also given me gifts to support and lead my family—and what am I doing? I'm modeling to a young boy every day how a man should act. I model to my daughter the man I eventually want her to be with. I serve my wife and uplift her. I want to show up every day 100% for them. They are everything to me.

By concentrating on what I thought I lost, I was resisting an opportunity to serve and encourage those around me. I was resisting one of my most considerable gifts: my efforts to put everything in my day toward benefiting the closest people in my life and my efforts to amplify my ability to serve others a hundredfold through my platforms. The better I get at this kind of work, the more people I can reach. I just had to remember—it's not about me!

Especially through these times of COVID, so many people are waking up to the awareness that "man, that vision I thought I had isn't quite as clear anymore." If you feel that way, I would like to encourage you. We've all been given gifts in our lives. If you know what your gifts are, start giving them away! Start using them for other people. If you don't know what your gifts are, remember question 3, and ask someone who cares about you. They'll be quick to tell you because other people can see the gifts in you. It will be obvious to them.

Serve your spouse, your parents, your families, and try to have an impact on people for the best. Spread as much joy as you can and watch the positivity fill up your life. Once you get outside yourself, it's a game-changer. The instant you start using your gifts to serve other people, your whole life and the lives of those you care about will completely change.

If your goals are to make more money, that's okay! Kyle Wilson once said, "If you want to be successful, bring value to the public. If you want to be wealthy, bring value to valuable people."

Who can you bring value to using the gifts that God has given you? Who are the most "valuable" people to you? Find out how you can serve those individuals, and you will start to find value in your own life, and the ancillary benefit could be a tremendous amount of success coming your way.

Honestly, you have to get outside of yourself first.

Adversity Is a Gift

Mac likes to say that "adversity is a gift." Part of what he means is that many of our supposed setbacks can help us change our perspective— which is one of the best ways to help us grow. Our setbacks can teach us so much about ourselves and give us another opportunity to share our gifts with others.

It certainly isn't easy, though. Adversity seems like the enemy because so often it changes things you feel are essential to you. If doctors could have miraculously healed my injury and I had been able to continue playing football, I would have taken that opportunity in a heartbeat. But would that actually have been better for my family and me?

Looking at it now from a different perspective, I'm not so sure. I could have been injured worse, perhaps even paralyzed. Or maybe I would have had a long, illustrious career, and it still would have eventually ended. You can't play football forever. And if you're lucky enough to be still playing into middle age, you're at risk for all kinds of long-term side effects from potential head injuries and wrecking your body for years. Being on the offensive line is brutal, and more than a few times, I'd felt like I've been run over by a freight train.

Potential concerns about my health aside, I also wouldn't have met some of the most incredible people in my life. I've received guidance from some of the best of humanity: spiritual leaders, masters of self-development, business tycoons, fellow athletes, and musical artists. I am humbled by what they have taught me and how they have expanded my life and perspective tremendously.

Highly regarded performance coach and keynote speaker Jordan Montgomery said, "God often packages our preparation as pain." We must realize that if we can examine the pain that we are suffering or have suffered in life, that oftentimes it's those moments that are preparing us for our what's next moment. That trauma will be the fuel or the experience that you need to be able to serve others.

When you are in the middle of a setback, your perspective is everything to not let it tank you. In Chapter 3, I'll talk about how to look at things in a way that is useful and can benefit you when adversity strikes. No matter how long your list of personal misfortunes (trust me, I had a *very* long list of personal disasters), you will find something valuable you can learn from and be grateful for.

Key Takeaways

Let's step back a bit and look at what we've covered so far:

- You have a full slate of natural gifts that you've used all your life.
- Your gifts will continue to serve you as you get to the next step.
- If you don't know what some of your gifts are, ask the following questions:
  1. What are you good at naturally?
  2. What have you learned to do well?
  3. What do people who love you say your gifts are?
  4. What are you resisting?
- Using your gifts to serve others and affect their lives will lift you up and make you more successful as well.
- Adversity is a gift that can reveal more of your other gifts.

3 Choose a Greater Perspective

Things don't happen to you. They happen for you.

—Ed Mylett

One of the biggest challenges in life is to see beyond the adversity that life throws at us from nearly the moment we start breathing. Having a greater sense of perspective and learning how to interpret and use adversity in a positive way will fundamentally improve your quality of life. Success is nearly impossible without this skill.

It's not like we can dodge bad things happening. Like death and taxes, adversity will always come at us one way or the other. As a center, I was used to adversity coming at me in a very physical, concrete way all the time (usually in the form of a defensive lineman directly engaging me in hand-to-hand combat)!

On the subject of adversity continually occurring in life, a great friend of mine, the University of Louisville FCA (Fellowship of Christian Athletes) director Chris Morgan, would always say, "In life, you're either in a storm, coming out of a storm, or heading into a storm."

That's an interesting way to look at it, and if you think about it, it makes sense. When you're not in a storm, it's crucial to appreciate the good times and understand that at some point, you'll be heading into one. If you're in the midst of a storm, know that this moment will pass, and eventually, you'll be coming out of it. And if you're about to head into a storm, you must shore up your gifts and your strengths to establish a foundation under you to help prepare you to weather it. For me, that's faith, family, friends, and a positive mindset—the strong foundation that has supported me in some of my most difficult trials.

What exactly do I mean by a positive mindset? I would describe it as taking anything thrown at you and figuring out how to make it work for you. One person who excels in this area, and has taught me a lot about having a greater perspective, is my friend Ed Mylett.

Ed Mylett is an incredible guy—a business leader, an expert on peak performance, and one of the top global keynote speakers in the world. I admired Ed Mylett for a long time before I ever met him personally. He also has a terrific podcast, "The Ed Mylett Show," which is the number 1 business podcast on iTunes.

Ed has a famous quote on perspective: "Things don't happen to you, they happen for you." That is an extremely powerful way of looking at life, because with this perspective, everything happens for a reason. Another way of saying it is that whatever happens to you, it isn't God or the universe conspiring against you. It's actually conspiring for your benefit.

It can be tricky to see things this way, especially in the middle of a big transition when you might feel that there's nothing good about what's happening to you. When I had the privilege of having Ed as a guest on my podcast (Episode 68: Max Out Your Life with Ed Mylett), he gave me a compelling example from his personal life when he was growing up.

I said, "Okay, I got one for you. How did having an alcoholic father happen *for* you?'" His dad was, I believe, 30 years sober before passing, but when he was growing up, he was a severe alcoholic. I was genuinely curious. I just wanted to know, "How did that happen *for* you?" I could think of some adversity I faced in my life, and I had a hard time imagining the upside of them. I'm sure you have something in your life that you feel the same way about.

Ed said that when he was a kid, he never knew which form of his father would walk through that front door. He had to learn how to read his father's face and emotions and body language the first few seconds he walked in and then adapted accordingly. From there, he learned how to "read" people based on his experience reading his dad.

Ed's experience reminded me of someone else. Famous author Malcolm Gladwell refers to a 10,000-hour rule in his book *Outliers*. Gladwell says, "Ten thousand hours is the magic number of greatness" (p. 40). In other words, if you spend 10,000 hours practicing nearly anything, I guarantee you'll be one of the best in the world at that skill.

So now, Ed has easily logged over 10,000 hours reading people very early in life, which enabled him to excel in podcasting, speaking, and selling and shine in the business world because he can read someone he's working with as well as he can read a crowd.

I thought it was incredible for him to talk about the takeaway he got from dealing with his father as a child. It was a way of taking something negative in his life and transmuting it into a skill that he could use to serve others. I thought, if he could feel this way about setbacks in his life, I could adopt his way of looking at some of the setbacks in mine.

What Ed was saying about things happening "for him" resonated because it felt familiar and right to me—I, too, have found the upside of so many events that would have completely derailed me if I let them.

I made a list and want to share with you how to find new ways of looking at the setbacks in your own life. It isn't a comprehensive list—I handpicked the ones from which I felt I learned the most.

Setback 1: Not Succeeding in Football Until Late in High School

I wasn't a starter on my high school varsity football team until my senior year. I don't know how many guys eventually ended up playing professional football with barely any experience from high school, but I'm probably one of the rare few. I'm sure many people thought I arrived way too late to the party to be considered seriously.

On its face, it looks to be a tremendous disadvantage going into college with so little experience. These other guys who had played a lot in high school were already thousands of hours ahead of me in terms of their experience, and that can be a little intimidating when you're starting out.

Positive Perspective 1: I Wasn't Hurt or Burned Out

For one, I was less banged up and injured than the other guys. I played with many guys in college—and obviously, a lot of them were four-year starters on the varsity football team. I was only a one-year starter, but the more years you play high-level football, the more you're going to get banged up. That's just football.

I had never been hurt at all playing football up to that point in my life. And a lot of it was because I only played one season. When you haven't been hurt yet, there's fresh energy and optimism to your game, a certain kind of fearlessness. There's also zero burnout. Many people have been playing the same position their whole life, and they get a little burned out on football by the time they get to college. Not me. I poured all that into my newfound enthusiasm for the game, which translated into disciplined practice.

Positive Perspective 2: I Was Grateful and Coachable

Because I hadn't played offensive line for more than a year, I didn't have any preconceived ideas about "the right way" to play the game.

I was too busy learning the basics and putting in everything I had into training to keep up with people more experienced than I was. Ego wasn't a factor—I hadn't played enough even to develop an ego about how I needed to play.

Plus, I was so grateful and appreciative of just being on the field! I had worked hard to get there, sacrificing basketball my junior year and training on a crazy level to put on 55 pounds. I would do everything and anything to not only stay but be considered one of the most valuable assets out there.

I also didn't have any bad habits. I didn't have time to develop any yet! So when I started playing center, I hadn't brought any bad habits to college with me. I purposely kept an open mind and wanted to learn the most effective ways to do my job on the team.

I was a sponge. I was incredibly coachable and listened to all the training and feedback my coach, trainers, and peers were giving me. With this frame of mind, I was able to create and reinforce positive habits.

My new positive habits paid off. I went from being a one-year starter in high school with one scholarship offer to being a Freshman All-American in college.

Setback 2: My Joe Theismann Leg Break

If you don't know what the Joe Theismann leg break is, let me give you some context. It's considered one of the most brutal moments ever televised in the NFL. In November 1985 the Redskins were playing against the Giants. Joe Theismann was the well-respected quarterback for the Redskins. In the first quarter of the game, Theismann was attempting a pass when two Giants defenders rushed him from opposite sides. Theismann tried to evade but was tackled from behind by Giants linebacker Lawrence Taylor.

Theismann's leg snapped in two, with both bones below his knee poking through the skin. Some of the other players said they could hear the snapping sound from the sidelines. It was a compound fracture of his tibia and fibula. The entire incident was televised live on *Monday Night Football*, and everyone watching witnessed the horrifying experience. Lawrence Taylor, the player who tackled him, was the first to wave the medical staff onto the field.

Theismann eventually recovered six months later, training and doing rehabilitation to return to the Redskins. Unfortunately, his injured leg healed shorter than before the injury, which gave him a bit of a hobble. There was no way he could play football after that.

Interestingly, the incident made the left tackle position famous because people had to adapt to protect the blind side of the quarterback once they realized that Lawrence Taylor was wrecking quarterbacks (and Joe Theismann's career). Most quarterbacks are right-handed, so they can't see the rushers coming off their left side as they drop back.

Theismann was as tough as they came and worked so hard to rehabilitate himself to playing condition, but, unfortunately, it wasn't enough. If a player ever gets the Theismann leg break, they know that it's terrible news. It's likely to be a career-ending injury.

My unfortunate incident happened my rookie year in week 12. We were playing down in Jacksonville. It was in November, and I had started every game that season, and I started every game through college, so, I never really had been hurt before. I was playing through nicks and bumps and bruises a lot of times, maybe some sprains and strains, but I always could get back out on the field and play.

In the third quarter, a former teammate of mine from the University of Louisville, Montavious Stanley, dove for our quarterback, Ryan Fitzpatrick. I was engaged and blocking my guy, and while I was in front of him, Montavious missed the quarterback and went through my left leg. I felt a sharp pain and immediately went down.

Because I had never been hurt before, I was unfamiliar with staying down on the ground after a play. It was the first time I ever did it, and so I actually tried to push myself up, and I heard Montavious start to cry—he was wailing once he realized that he broke my leg so severely.

I just laid there, and eventually, teammates and trainers helped put me on a cart. They put my leg in an air cast, put me in a cart, took me off the field, and went straight into an ambulance. Funny thing—I watched the YouTube video of my leg getting broken before going into the operating room. I watched it with the surgeons when they were trying to see what happened; the whole play was already on YouTube.

As far as broken bones went, this was pretty serious. I wasn't going anywhere anytime soon. I was stuck down in Jacksonville for four days. I was able to fly back home to Buffalo only after about a week of being in the hospital there,

That was the first time I'd ever been seriously hurt before, and fighting back from that was a daily struggle. There were so many bad days along the way.

Positive Perspective 1: I Became Much Closer with My Girlfriend and Future Wife

Back then, Leslie and I had been dating about a year. She dropped out of school to move in with me and take care of me when I returned to Buffalo from Jacksonville. I can't even tell you how lucky I was to have her in my life. I got to experience her as a caregiver, and she was terrific at it. I'm not sure words can express how grateful I was for all the work she put into helping rehabilitate me. It was instrumental to my recovery.

When you're younger, you might start a relationship with a girl because she's pretty, and you keep dating her because she's fun and you get along with her. But when you marry a girl, you don't know what type of mom and wife she will be once kids come around.

I got to see Leslie's nurturing side, and she truly took care of me when I could do nothing for myself—including using the restroom. It was not ideal to have the girl you're dating to have to empty a urine jug every time you have to pee. It was inconvenient and maybe even embarrassing, but she had an "I got this" attitude.

I saw her in a new light early on in our relationship, which gave me a lot of assurance about who she was as a person. I proposed not long after because I knew I needed to marry this girl. She stuck by me at my worse and sacrificed everything to help me. It was one of the best and easiest decisions of my life.

Positive Perspective 2: I Proved to Myself That I Could Fight Back from Catastrophic Injury

The Theismann injury took me out of the rest of that first season. I put hard-disciplined work into my rehabilitation because it was my goal to get back out on the football field for that second year. It was the injury that ended Joe Theismann's career—I didn't want it to finish mine.

It was a time in my life when I had to shore up my strongest gifts and put them to use. I would need to call on my competitive spirit and self-discipline to give it my all in rehab. It's a strange feeling, putting so much effort and pain into doing something you have taken for granted nearly all your life: walking. You never realize how many things in your body have to be working in perfect order simply to get up and walk across the room.

I knew that the training room was where I would win the next few years of football battles. I wouldn't be able to do it unless I built the proper foundation now. I needed to give it all here in rehab and leave nothing on the table.

It was a long road back to recovery and battling through a rehab process for such a serious injury. For the first time in my life, I was able to prove to myself at that moment how much football meant to me by pushing through all the pain and long days in the training room.

When you go through something like that and come out the other side healed, it changes you. I had confidence that I could come back from significant injury, great adversity, and be stronger than ever. I proved to myself I could do it, and that's a fantastic thing that came out of that injury.

Positive Perspective 3: I Appreciated Being Pain-Free and Felt the Joy of Playing at Such a High Level Again

I did finally make it back. It wasn't pretty at first. It's one thing to walk and run after recovering from the Theismann break. It's quite another to be playing football with other top athletes out there, running and blocking at peak capacity. There were many times when I was hobbling around the field, not really at my best. I played pretty crappy that year, honestly, worse than I ever envisioned myself playing in an NFL game.

Once I got back to moving and playing pain-free, I truly appreciated being out there and running around and playing at a high level again. Without that injury, I may have taken for granted what an incredible blessing it is to play professional sports with some of the best in the world. I don't think I would have treasured it the same way had I never gotten hurt and gone through those really tough times of rehabbing my way back to the field.

Setback 3: My MCL Injury

In my fourth year, I tore my MCL during a game against Jacksonville that we won. The MCL is a ligament in the knee, similar to what had happened to me before with the ACL during my third year in the NFL, just not as severe.

I honestly just started examining everything in my life. I was exceptionally frustrated—I got hurt all four years to start my career with the Bills. I had played 49 consecutive games in Louisville and barely had a scratch. I started just analyzing everything. I thought, "I'm getting hurt every single season. Is God trying to tell me something? Am I training correctly? Am I not eating correctly?"

I knew I had to change something, starting with my perspective of how I could use this injury to get back on top.

Positive Perspective 1: By Taking Responsibility for the Conditions That Led to My Injury, I Could Empower Myself to Change It

Sometimes you have to divorce yourself from the emotions you're feeling from a setback and look at the valuable learning you can gain from it. Perhaps you've done something a certain way all your life, and now all of a sudden, it stops working. If you're getting uncomfortable feedback in the form of multiple setbacks, it's a good idea to look back at the basics. What can I switch up to improve the situation? What no longer works and why?

That was the "a-ha" moment I got out of this injury—I had to take responsibility for it. There's a double-edged sword to taking responsibility for what happens to you. But the wonderful part of it is that once you take responsibility for something, you have the power to change it.

So, I knew I had to change something. I just felt like something was off. So I switched up how I was training during the season. The NFL season is so long, and many people just try to maintain strength throughout the year. I think in trying just to maintain my strength, I was probably getting weaker, which led me to play weaker toward the end of the season.

After I completely changed my training strategy, I went on to start 52 straight games—the most consecutive games started for any active center in the NFL at the time.

Positive Perspective 2: I Had a Golden Opportunity to Demonstrate My Commitment to My Coaches and Teammates by Fighting Back

After I tore my MCL, there were only four games left in the regular season. I was heading into the final year of my rookie contract after this season, which was likely going to be my biggest payday as an NFL player.

At this point, we were eliminated from the playoffs, but that didn't matter to me. If I had gone on injured reserved (IR) and ended the season right there, everyone would have understood. I knew I was taking a risk by going out to play—I could potentially risk an even worse injury. We were not making the playoffs, so that wasn't at stake. Many people would have completely understood if I had just shut it down for the rest of the year.

I just didn't want to do it. I had been on IR for two out of three years of the start of my career. I wanted to fight back. But I also wanted to prove to the organization what I was all about. I wanted to show them that I was the kind of player willing to play through some pain, and if I was medically able to go out there and play, I wanted to prove to the Buffalo Bills' organization that I would do it whole-heartedly.

That's precisely what I did. I felt like that was the right way to close out that season, and I think I earned a lot of respect from coaches and teammates going out there. I proved to them playing in those final two games that I was willing to go all out and put it all on the line. I proved it to myself, too.

Before the next season, the Bills ended up rewarding me with a contract that would create generational wealth for my family and me.

It was an incredible reward and fantastic recognition for all the work. I was so profoundly grateful. I think part of the reason for the terms of that contract was me battling back from all of those injuries, but especially going out and playing those two meaningless games of the last season.

Is there an area in your life that you can push through some discomfort to show commitment to your work or your relationships? Going above and beyond for a period of time in your life can dramatically change the course of your life—even if your circumstances seem bleak at the time.

Setback 4: The Career-Ending Neck Injury

In Chapter 1, I wrote about all I went through during the events surrounding that neck injury. With the passage of time and a reflection on my strengths, gifts, and family, I have been able to step back and see what had happened from a greater perspective.

Positive Perspective 1: I Ended My Football Career on a Career-High Note

So many things went right that last season. We had finally broken the playoff drought, and I could leave on a high note. We came together with tremendous teamwork, leadership, and commitment from the whole organization. I could not have been happier with those results.

Positive Perspective 2: Our Family Was Financially Set

I signed a contract extension before the start of the season, which was very good for my family and me financially. We had just built our dream house in Louisville, which checked all the boxes for where we wanted to live and raise our kids. It's beautiful here—I love our home so much.

Positive Perspective 3: I Was Able to Spend More Time with My Family

Garrett was just born. I had this healthy son, and now I was able to spend a lot of time with him, my daughter, and my wife in an incredible environment. I always like to say, "God's timing is perfect," and Garrett arriving when he did was a perfect example of that.

Not everyone has the blessing of spending so much time with their family. We are all growing in amazing ways together. I am grateful that I can be close to my wife and kids for this incredible next chapter in our lives.

Positive Perspective 4: I Can Take Care of My Body for the Long Term

I love football so much. I would have probably played until the wheels fell off, to the point where I was extremely broken. Maybe it was God's way of getting me out of the game yet still allowing me to be active. I can still play golf with my friends and do a little bit of wake surfing and some low-impact activities, so I can still be physical without risking my neck at all.

My health journey is never finished. I'll talk further about my efforts to lose weight, my experiments with running, and my long-term efforts to reverse the potential long-term damage I have done through all my seasons in football in Chapter 6. The short version of the story is that I'm grateful to be on the right track and improve demonstrably in almost every way.

You're never too old to reverse course and start living in a more healthy, mindful way to increase your quality of life and longevity.

Positive Perspective 5: It Gave Me a Podcasting Platform and Story to Help Other People Transition

Possibly the reason so many people listen to my podcast is that I had this huge, life-changing event—the career-ending injury—right when

I thought everything was going so perfectly. That season gave me a platform that has changed my life and allowed me to have an impact on others.

I always come back to, "How am I using my gifts to serve others?" If I can inform the listeners, if I can uplift them, if I can provide them some entertainment within their day, I can bring them a little bit more joy in their life. I know I'm serving them through this podcast and my broadcasts.

I've talked about how your biggest test becomes your testimony at that point in your life. Your testimony is your story of conversion that can inspire others. That was my biggest test. I just thought, "Well, here we go. God gave me this platform amidst all this adversity. Let's do something extremely powerful with it."

Ways to Shift Your Perspective When You're Stuck

Therapists are known to say that you can't control the events that happen to you in life, but you can control how you react to them. I believe this is true.

I have another take on it—you can only control two things when major setbacks in life occur: what you pay attention to and what meaning you give it.

If I had paid attention to the wrong thing or assigned some meaning that it didn't need, I could have sunk myself in any of my setbacks. The most dramatic example—if I had made my career-ending neck injury mean that I was useless or no longer had any contribution to make to society, then my life would have followed accordingly.

The Power of Gratitude

Another thing that helped me tremendously during that time, especially after the birth of my son, is that I took stock of my life and was grateful for everything I had.

It didn't mean I wasn't devastated that I couldn't play football anymore. It meant that I had a profound sense of gratitude for the things that I did have—my family, my faith, my incredible network of support, and the success I had accrued so far.

Author Jon Gordon said in "The Power of Thank You," "It's actually physiologically impossible to be stressed and thankful at the same time. When you are grateful, you flood your body and brain with emotions and endorphins that uplift and energize you rather than the stress hormones that drain you. Gratitude and appreciation are also essential for a healthy work environment."

Gratitude is a practice you can work at every day. And you'll find the more you practice gratitude, the more you'll find yourself having things to be grateful for. Take stock of everything that's working, the fantastic people in your life, and all the things headed in the right direction.

Moving for Perspective

When you're still having a hard time seeing a different vantage point, I recommend shifting your attitude by moving your body or shifting your breathing.

There's a lot to be said about just changing your state through movement. Whether it's a run and a workout, hitting some golf balls, or doing anything physical. Maybe you can practice breathing exercises. There are many different techniques, but there's a lot of science behind using breathing to change your mental and emotional state.

Another great thing you can do is to literally go somewhere else and physically see a different perspective. If you are stuck in the same place all the time, it's challenging to think outside the four walls in which you have been spending all your time. Get out and literally change your perspective—see much more of the landscape. For some people, that means going to a lake, river, or ocean. Maybe you can take a drive and see a view from a higher place, like a hill or mountain. Perhaps it's just simply heading out into nature and listening to the silence or the noises in your natural environment.

Reach Out and Get Help from Others

You are not alone! Your elders, your family, your mentors, your colleagues, and friends—they have all fought and won battles you know nothing about. Talking to someone else is a great way to shift your perspective and start seeing alternatives you may have never considered before.

When you're in a tough spot in life, you'll be surprised at how much compassion those who are farther along on their journey can give you and what great wisdom they have to offer. They might have some tough advice to give you along the way. It's amazing, in those times when you're the most vulnerable about your struggles (whether it's how much pain you're in or a financial situation or a struggling relationship), how compassionate people can be.

You may also want to consider professional therapy, which, thankfully over the years, has become more socially acceptable in the mainstream. It's a great way of dealing with issues that you may feel are too big to handle yourself.

Consider That All the Trials You Face Make You Stronger and More Complete

One of my favorite Bible verses on this subject comes from James 1:2–4: "Consider it pure joy, my brothers and sisters, whenever you face trials of many kinds, because you know that the testing of your faith produces perseverance. Let perseverance finish its work so that you may be mature and complete, not lacking anything."

If you take the perspective that everything you face strengthens and prepares you for the future, it can lessen the sting of the situation you are dealing with in the present.

Key Takeaways

Let's reflect for a moment and think of the key takeaways we have so far:

- "Things don't happen to you. They happen for you" (courtesy Ed Mylett).
- Having a greater sense of perspective and learning how to interpret and use adversity in a positive way will fundamentally improve your quality of life.
- Success is nearly impossible without seeing a greater perspective.
- Practicing adopting a greater perspective makes you better at it. (Remember the 10,000-hour rule!)
- Great things can still come out of horrible circumstances.
- Losing one thing often makes room for other things.
- It's okay to feel bad about things that have happened.
- You only have control of what you pay attention to and the meaning you give it.
- Find ways to take stock and be grateful.
- When stuck, get moving and breathe differently!
- Take yourself out of your environment regularly to literally see a different perspective.
- Reach out and get help from others.
- Understand that all the trials you face makes you stronger.

4 Create a Vision for Your Future

The bottom line is that if you're serious about creating a new future, then you better be engaged in the process of creating a vision of the future, because if you're not, then that just means you're more in love with your past than you are with your future.

—Dr. Joe Dispenza

When I was a professional athlete, my professional "vision" was never a question. We wanted to be the best team possible, we wanted to win, and we wanted to go all the way to achieve a victory in the Super Bowl. Every minute of every day was designed, scheduled, and executed for that purpose.

However, I was also learning more profound distinctions for vision, like how to visualize my success in a way that would actually make it happen. I could create the vision and break it down into smaller steps. If I could see it, really see it in my mind's eye, then I knew I had a better chance of actualizing it on the field. This skill was part of our training as players.

The Bills brought in a performance coach who introduced us to specific visualization exercises before my last season in the NFL. He spoke to our team about the power of visualization and how you only have so much time and energy to put in your football reps, but you can exercise those reps even further in your mind. Essentially, you can take extra reps through visualization exercises where you're not taxing your body anymore, and you can benefit from the mental practice of these exercises.

I'm a huge golfing fan, and one of my favorite players, Jack Nicklaus, said, "I never hit a shot, not even in practice, without having a very sharp in-focus picture of it in my head."

Many celebrities who rise to the top of their fields in sports, entertainment, and the arts all say essentially the same thing: visualization works. From Jim Carrey to Tiger Woods, from Oprah Winfrey to Einstein, to Steve Harvey to Muhammed Ali—the list goes on and on.

So how and why does it work? Ask a poet or a theologian, and you might get a different answer. I personally believe that there is some degree of divinity involved—that it may be like God answering a prayer. That's a matter of faith—and if that's not enough for some people, the science is overwhelming and persuasive.

Writer A. J. Adams wrote an excellent article for *Psychology Today* on the topic called "Seeing Is Believing: The Power of Visualization." She writes specifically about how visualization works in the brain:

Brain studies now reveal that thoughts produce the same mental instructions as actions. Mental imagery impacts many cognitive processes in the brain: motor control, attention, perception, planning, and memory. So, the brain is getting trained for actual performance during visualization. It's been found that mental practices can enhance motivation, increase confidence and self-efficacy, improve motor performance, prime your brain for success, and increase states of flow—all relevant to achieving your best life!

What an incredible thing. If you practice visualizing an action, you get almost the same benefits as if you are actually doing it. The performance coach we were working with that last football season really got my wheels going about all the different ways to use visualization to improve my game.

And that's one of the reasons I think it's essential that you adopt a greater perspective (like I discussed in Chapter 3) before you start to visualize. If your thoughts are too negative, they will tax your mind and body as if they had physically happened. Are you practicing failing and fear over and over again in your mind? Or are you practicing the best outcome?

Your thoughts become your actions, and your actions become your habits, and your habits create your future. So, you have to be incredibly careful with your thoughts. You can shift your whole reality just based on the thoughts that you're intentionally creating. Our brains are incredible gifts with power that we are only beginning to understand.

I thought about my position as the center and asked myself what was my most challenging time in a game and how could I make those times easier through visualization? I took it so far to imagine myself in different NFL stadiums. I had to get super specific. It wasn't just how I was playing—it was *where*. So if I were going to play in Jacksonville for the next game, I would imagine the stadium in Jacksonville. If I had never played in whatever stadium was coming up, I would look up a YouTube video to examine what the stadium looks and feels like.

I would even visualize the people I was going against, study film on them, and imagine countering their every move. As I said before, these guys are defensive geniuses who can sometimes trick you. They know you've studied them, so sometimes they appear to do one of their signature plays to confuse you when in reality, they are practicing an entirely different strategy. I would visualize how to beat them in that circumstance, too.

Specificity and repetition were essential when I practiced these visualizations. I would sit at the edge of my bed, take some deep breaths, and use my imagination to take me there and fill in anything and everything I could conceivably think of. I would visualize everything down to whether it was a night game or a day game and what the crowd would be like. And then I visualized myself getting the job done.

There are so many benefits to visualization. It is incredible how much more calm and in control you feel when you find yourself in situations you have already visualized in advance. You can make better and more effective decisions about what to do and not get caught like a deer in the headlights.

For a time, I felt like I had a handle on using vision and visualization and how to make it work for me. Everything felt like it made sense, and it was a matter of perfecting what I was already working toward. And then—then my football career was over.

I was faced with a new problem. How would I use vision if I didn't know where I was going, what I was doing, or what I wanted anymore?

That was the new challenge.

Seeing Past the Moment

What I didn't know was how to create a vision out of nothing when everything seemed blown apart. How do you create a big enough future for yourself when your present seems so small? And how do you make new frontiers in your mind when you are overwhelmed by the setbacks of the past?

There's nothing wrong with you if you feel overwhelmed or stuck in a moment and are unsure how to climb your way out. Much of this has to do with human biology and psychology. Once you know what's going on, you can climb your way out. I've seen people get trapped in their circumstances so often, unable to see their greater future. I've been there myself. If thoughts became reality, I was in danger of losing so much of the momentum that I had built.

When bad things happen to you, your body and mind go through a natural physiological fight or flight (or freeze) response. The response is an instinctive reaction meant to protect us and has helped our ancestors evade predators or survive in life-and-death situations since ancient times.

I've learned much from the writing of Dr. Joe Dispenza, an author, researcher, lecturer, and corporate consultant who works with people to "make measurable changes in their lives." Much of his research is in the fields of neuroscience and neuroplasticity. Neuroplasticity is the ability of the brain to grow and adapt its neural networks. Studies have shown that neural networks are strengthened by practice, and new practices can form new neural networks.

Dr. Dispenza says that this human instinct often gets in the way of seeing a greater vision. When we reach our pivot point, that moment where we're not sure how we're going to go on, or if we are uncertain about how we will survive, that's when we are the most vulnerable to sabotaging our futures. Dispenza says in his blog "Getting Clear on Your Vision":

Because we can't take care of our basic survival needs, **we have difficulty believing a new future is possible**. Why then would we dream of anything bigger? It's because the cocktail of chemicals derived from the hormones of stress causes us to narrow our focus on matter and objects in our immediate world (that's where the danger and threats are), and we stop thinking about future potentials and possibilities. And so doubt begins to clog the vision.

As Dr. Dispenza says, "When we're in survival mode, nature has taught us that it's not a time to create—it's time to run, fight, or hide. Why dream of anything bigger if we can't get past our current self? This leads to stagnation and resignation."

There is a way out when you feel like this. You have to speak (or write) a new perspective or a new vision into existence. It has to come from you—new hopes and dreams based on your desire and imagination. Writing, learning, speaking, and imagining are the essential ingredients to see a different future for yourself.

Your future is bigger than your past! If you're not actively creating a future, you may not like where your future takes you.

Contemplate and Write Down Your Thoughts and Feelings

It's not pie-in-the-sky thinking to create a new future for yourself. However, it does require some work to get a positive perspective first and do serious self-reflection or contemplation. Meditation, journaling, quiet time, exercise, spending time in nature, and prayer are all great methods to get more in touch with yourself and visualize a future for yourself based on a more positive perspective.

Uncertain times are an excellent reminder to get back to yourself and spend more quiet time, which is valuable for learning a lot about yourself and maybe even receiving higher wisdom. In the morning, after I finish my inspirational reading, I practice a time of silence that's a combination of prayer and visioning my day going well, and who I want to be that day, with some affirmations. I'll say to myself,

"You are positive. You are making an impact. God has a plan, and you can trust his plans for your life."

I've also experimented with many different types of meditation. I think all of them are valuable, and I think time in prayer or silence is also helpful.

You don't know how much you're missing out on your inner wisdom or God speaking to you when you don't have moments of true silence in your life. I think that is a particular problem in modern life, the way we live wirelessly with all these devices. It used to be people could get little doses of quiet time wherever they were: waiting in line, waiting for the bus, in between activities at home.

You need to leave room for silence—it's really just making room for yourself. And you then can make room for visualization.

I came across a great article from *Scientific American* in 2013 titled "Why Your Brain Needs More Downtime" by Ferris Jabr. It argues that there is scientific proof that little moments of quiet are necessary for the brain to thrive. Jabr writes:

Downtime replenishes the brain's stores of attention and motivation, encourages productivity and creativity, and is essential to both achieve our highest levels of performance and simply form stable memories in everyday life. **A wandering mind unsticks us in time so that we can learn from the past and plan for the future.** Moments of respite may even be necessary to keep one's moral compass in working order and maintain a sense of self.
[Emphasis is mine.]

Jabr also writes that "epiphanies may seem to come out of nowhere, but they are often the product of unconscious mental activity during downtime." It's a great point. You're just not going to get the same flashes of insight if you spend every free moment you have surfing the net, scrolling, or watching YouTube videos.

One of the little epiphanies I got from my personal reflection was that I was surrounded by people who would uplift me. My family and close friends have all been incredibly supportive. They gave me a positive perspective early on. And let's be honest, I was very lucky I had this healthy, happy family. And I was lucky I was still healthy and moving around. I wasn't lying paralyzed with loss of respiratory function, which was the reality I was looking at with damage at the spinal cord where my injury occurred.

I needed to do a lot of contemplation and perspective on my end so that I didn't just wake up every day and say, "Man, this stinks. I can't play football anymore." I took a page from Ed Mylett—things didn't happen to me; they happened for me. Now I get to do all of these things, and to keep it going there is a lot of perspective work that I still do personally to this day. Journaling and quiet prayer or a devotional at the beginning of the day is part of my morning routine.

Just like physical training or learning an instrument, reflection and contemplation work best if you practice them every day. Over time, you'll recognize things in your life you'd like to change and what things serve you that you should keep. As you steep in your wishes, feelings, complaints, and dreams, you'll start to see a bigger picture of where you want to go. From here, you can start building your vision of a more fantastic future.

Conquering Obstacles in the Way of Envisioning Your Ideal Self

So how do you see your ideal self or a greater vision for your life? Do you feel a bit of discomfort or mixed feelings when trying to picture it? If you do, that is entirely normal. Multiple feelings and thoughts come up for people through this process.

1: Perfectionism

Sometimes I think people are afraid to make a wrong move or do something that doesn't work out. Here's the thing—you can always change your mind. If you feel like you must be sure about every move before you make it, you will never make any moves at all. You can't do that on the football field, and you certainly can't do that in life, either. I feel it's important to get a sense of momentum. Perfectionism about your life can just be a form of procrastination.

2: Fear of Failure

Fear of failure is hazardous and insidious because it also can prevent you from doing anything at all. For some people, the fear of failing has more power over them than actually failing. In football and sports in general, we love to win and hate to lose.

Throughout the first half of my career, fear of failure took a lot of the joy out of playing football for me. I was constantly worried about getting hurt again or not playing at a level that justified my first-round draft pick status. Once I got over the fear of failing and simply let it loose each Sunday, the game was so much more enjoyable to play, and I actually played a lot better.

Often, our fear of failure comes from worrying about what others will say or think about us falling short. Block out that noise and simply commit to your daily process of discipline and commitment, and then you can live with the results however they fall. Nothing of value in life comes without challenge or risk. Embrace the challenge and when you do fail, learn from it and get better from it!

3: Dwelling on the Immediate Past

Then there's the issue of something I call *negative momentum*, when you might make a mistake and then let your thoughts dwell on that mistake, screwing up the present. This gives your immediate past more power than your future.

I'll give you an example. Coming from college to the NFL, I experienced a little bit of culture shock. In college, I was used to being among the best. There were some games where I played against somebody who would never beat me one time an entire game, and I was just a better player. But when I got to the NFL, those guys were the best of the best. I wasn't used to being outplayed. Early in my career, I would get so hot on the sidelines and so upset if I ever got beat. I'd often throw my helmet when I got to the sideline—which is embarrassing.

I remember something Geoff Hangartner, our center when I was playing guard next to him my rookie year, said to me that had a big impact on my career. He said, "You know, Eric, those guys get paid, too. They're going to beat you sometimes, and it's okay, but you can't let one bad play compound into more bad plays."

4: Impostor Syndrome

Another thing that comes up a lot, even for me, is impostor syndrome. That's when you feel you are unqualified or unworthy of a particular title, accomplishment, or gift. For example, I might say to myself, "Who am I to write a book? I've never done that before." This is uncomfortable for me to admit because I'm a natural extrovert—I love affecting people. I love leading. But there was this underlying imposter syndrome that haunted me for the longest time. It was my executive coach, Mac, who encouraged me to write a book and wanted me to start doing more speaking. I had to conquer a lot of my doubts about myself and just move forward. I learned later that this is a common problem, part of the human condition.

Keep in mind that having imposter syndrome is often a good thing. That means that you're stretching yourself outside your comfort zone. Embrace those feelings and understand that all the greats in your industry often felt those same feelings when they got started initially.

There are several antidotes to impostor syndrome. One is reminding yourself how much you have accomplished so far. Affirmations that reinforce your attitude and perception of your ability are also helpful. Talk to your friends or mentors—we often view ourselves more negatively than anyone else. Your friends can give you a countering perspective. And also, remember it's okay not to know what you're doing 100% of the time.

5: Fear of Accountability or Responsibility

Once people start to envision big futures for themselves, they have the hard work of holding themselves accountable for it. Maybe they feel like they have bitten off more than they can chew, and perhaps the prospect of working so hard to achieve the vision seems intimidating and full of responsibilities they may not want. It's a big job to fulfill your potential, and it takes a lot of courage to see it and go for it. It also means changing a lot of comfortable habits.

Let's face it, big visions or dreams require hard work. There's no mistake about that. However, the rewards of hard work are almost always worth it. Randy Pausch, a computer science professor at Carnegie Mellon University, had an interesting take on the idea of hard work and obstacles on the way to success. He was diagnosed with pancreatic cancer and given only a few months to live, so he decided to use the time he had left to inspire others, starting with a lecture that went viral called "The Last Lecture."

Pausch said, "The brick walls are there for a reason. The brick walls are not there to keep us out. The brick walls are there to give us a chance to show how badly we want something. Because the brick walls are there to stop the people who don't want it badly enough. They're there to stop the other people." Given my life experience, what he said resonated with me. How badly had I wanted to be a professional football player when I started? Bad enough to work harder at my craft than I could have imagined I could work.

I'm just passionate about being disciplined in life, and I know that will bear fruit, guaranteed. No matter what is going on in your life, if you have and exercise personal discipline, you'll prepare yourself for those big opportunities that you envision for yourself. When they come, you will be happy with the person you see in the mirror. Self-confidence comes from keeping the promises you make to yourself. It also comes from discipline—honoring the commitment to keep promises to yourself.

Key Takeaways

Here are some of the key takeaways we have so far:

- Your future is bigger than your past.
- Visualization is scientifically proven to improve your performance.
- Your mind gets nearly the same benefit from mentally practicing as from physical practicing.
- The more specific your vision is, the more effective it will be in helping you achieve it.
- You carry the most critical role in creating your future, not random circumstances.
- In moments of transition, it can be challenging to see past the bad circumstances.
- Quiet contemplation can help you get in touch with a bigger future, beyond the moment.

- Visualization is effective for small-scale and larger-scale visions.

- Your vision can always change—you don't have to have clarity about everything

- Many conquerable obstacles can come up when creating a greater vision for yourself:

  ◆ Perfectionism

  ◆ Fear of failure

  ◆ Dwelling on the immediate past

  ◆ Impostor syndrome

  ◆ Fear of accountability or responsibility

5 Examine Your Core Values

Your values create your internal compass that can navigate how you make decisions in your life. If you compromise your core values, you go nowhere.

—Roy T. Bennett, *The Light in the Heart*

Ever have that uneasy feeling that you are totally off course?

You know you're headed in the wrong direction, and maybe you're not even sure how you know that. But you feel it deep in your gut, and that uncomfortable feeling tells you something needs to change.

Compare that to the opposite feeling, when everything seems right. You feel like you have the wind at your back and you're sailing in the right direction. You may have challenges that come up. However, you feel you are entirely equipped to handle them.

The difference between these two vastly different feelings goes to the very essence of your *core values* and whether you live your life aligned with them.

So, what exactly do I mean by core values? They can be described in any number of ways—your sacred beliefs, the forces that drive you, a personal code of conduct. They are deeply held beliefs that you practice and use to live your everyday life. They define you as a person in the way that you live.

Having a strong, unshakeable sense of your core values dramatically affects how you deal with your pivot point. You will find yourself more resilient and able to withstand the impact of an unexpected emergency or disaster. If you do get knocked off course, it won't be for long because you have such a fundamental sense of yourself.

You also develop higher confidence in yourself. People who know their core values know precisely how to optimize their life to live within them. When they live aligned with their core values, they tend to be more successful, too. It's almost impossible not to be.

When you don't have a firm grip on your core values, you're in for a tough time. You may find yourself hanging out with people you don't like, doing things you don't really want to do, and feeling a ton of anxiety about it. You may feel stuck, or on a downturn, or angry or disgusted with yourself. You probably won't be performing anywhere near your best at any given task or vocation. The price of not being true to who you really are is outright misery.

The good news in this situation is that you can always shift course. You can adopt a new set of core values that more accurately reflect who you want to be, or you can finally start following the excellent set of core values that may have been there all along. It's never too late to turn around.

So, what if you don't know what your core values are?

Finding Your Core Values

I believe that most people have some idea about their highest priority beliefs and behaviors. However, as with most things, it's hard to be objective when you're right in the middle of it. Similar to your unique gifts, sometimes your friends have a clearer picture of your values than you do. Your core values are the upstream source of nearly all the positive ways you show up in the world. They come from your actions sourced from your beliefs. Your close friends and family will be able to see that.

Ask your friends and family questions: "How would you describe me to a stranger?" Or, "What are some of the reasons we are close friends?" Or another great one, "How have I positively affected you?" It's not an exercise in fishing for compliments. It's gathering needed feedback to get clear about how you want to show up in this world.

Another way to clear up your core values is to examine what your day-to-day living looks like. What is your vocation? Do you enjoy your work? How do you spend the day? How do you use your gifts? When do you feel at peace? When do you feel loved? What excites you? What gives you hope? Why do you get out of bed in the morning?

Sometimes you have to take behavior you observe in yourself and follow it upstream to the source, the core value. For example, say every morning you go jogging and eat a healthy breakfast. The behavior is exercise and good eating. Then just ask the magic question of "why?" *Why* are exercise and healthy eating important to you? Your answer might be, "I want to be healthy so I can live a long time." Or it might be, "I want to be as healthy as possible for my kids." Or maybe it's, "I want to be healthy so I can attract a mate and raise a family." Or perhaps, "I want to be healthy because my body is a temple, and I am honoring God." Your reasons for being healthy could be one or all of these things or any combination in between.

It's common to share a core value with others. For example, many people have some variation of a health core value in their lives. Values about family, love, helping others, and God are all very common, even though they differ in their type or specificity. We human beings, at the end of the day, all want very similar things.

So when we find ourselves in a spot where we don't feel right, one of the first places to look is whether or not we are aligned with our core values.

Getting Back into Alignment with Your Core Values

Sometimes you slip out of alignment with your core values. It doesn't make you a bad person—you can always turn things around. But I believe it is important to get back on the horse as soon as possible. That's why it's crucial to stay present and notice what's happening. When you are off your mark, the internal feelings you get are the first wave of feedback you need to change.

There is an example from my own life that I would love to share.

I had a lot of things go wrong my freshman year at the University of Louisville. One of the biggest surprises was my poor academic performance. In my first semester, I got a 2.7 GPA—well under my standards and far below what my parents expected of me. I could have done better, and I knew that.

In addition to that, I got mono, short for mononucleosis. It's not a serious condition, but it can last for months, and some of the symptoms are extreme fatigue, nausea, loss of appetite, and loss of muscle tone. All of that meant that I lost a lot of weight. Luckily, I was redshirting that year, still developing as a player, so I wouldn't play that season anyway. Still, my performance took a significant hit, and that's hard to take when you're used to playing at such a competitive level.

I think stumbling through that first semester academically, getting mononucleosis, having to sit out of our spring football because of that, and really missing being out in the field led to some changes in some values that I needed to establish.

So, later on in my freshman year, I went through some intense reflection because I wanted to turn things around. I would wake up early and go to work hard in the weight room. I thought to myself, "Hey, I'm on a four-year college scholarship. I could go in one of two directions. I can chase my dreams, or I can party hard and not make the most of this amazing opportunity.

I said to myself, "You know what I'm going to do? I'm going to go and maximize my gifts here." I'm a better student than that. I needed to start working harder. I needed to be more disciplined in the classroom. And I definitely needed to prioritize my health and sleep because I couldn't let my immune system go. My immune system was keeping me out of football, the thing I loved the most, which was the whole reason I was there! And had I been paying attention to my body, I probably never would have gotten mono in the first place.

One of the reasons I share that story is that we are vulnerable when we are down, and that's the perfect time to revisit our value system. We're all just now coming out of a deadly pandemic that has affected everyone through no fault of their own. People didn't do anything wrong to bring about this situation, yet some lost their jobs or loved ones.

When you already have a reinforced and clear sense of your core values, it makes being resilient and strong in these situations so much easier. It doesn't stop the storms in life from coming; you're just better prepared to weather the storm.

Seeking Others Who Model Core Values You Want

There were some things I needed to start taking seriously and get back to find the important things in my life. One of those things was my faith, identity as a Christian, and my relationship with God. At the University of Louisville, I started going to the Fellowship of

Christian Athletes (FCA) meetings, which helped me develop my relationship with Christ. At the time, only eight total athletes were attending.

Sometimes you recognize a core value in someone that you want to adopt. The person models it for you and makes you think, "I want to be like that." That's part of why I got into FCA to begin with. The FCA director, Chris Morgan, lived and modeled a way that was intriguing to me. He lived with a joy about him. He had a work ethic that separated him from those around him. It was all essentially stemming from a foundation in Christ, which I may or may not have recognized, but when people live a certain way, you want to follow what they do. I got to see what type of husband he was and what kind of father he was.

That inspired me. He was a leader worth following, and if Chris were really into anything, I probably would have followed him back then. He just so happened to be the leader of FCA at the time, and he remains an extremely close friend of mine. Years later, I'm on the FCA board now.

But at that time, it was a no-pressure environment, it was a simple invitation to join him, but those invitations were in the way he lived his life. Now I try to live a certain way that others would want to follow, whether inspiring people through a weight loss journey and a health journey, being a dad and a husband, or living with a certain amount of joy. Maybe it's living with discipline in my life. That's what I want to model.

Having an impact on and leading others to make their what's next in life their best yet is what drives my actions on a daily basis—understanding that I have now been given a platform from God through football and my other gifts.

Given your gifts, who in your life models the core values that you want? Is there someone in your life you follow because of their actions? Are you living in a way that others would want to follow you?

Define Your Hard Boundaries

Any person who works in the mental health field will tell you that solid boundaries are necessary to be mentally healthy. If you want to succeed at the game of life, you have to define your playing field and where you draw the line and say, "I won't cross this boundary."

If you are uncertain exactly of your core values, try determining your hard boundaries or non-negotiable areas and work backward from there. It might be easier to instinctively know what you aren't about, so you can deduce why.

When my football career ended, and I needed to lock down my core values before navigating to my next career path, here is where I started: What wasn't I willing to compromise? What boundary wouldn't I cross? What were my rules for life? I started going through some of my hard, non-negotiable boundaries and rules.

At the time, we were (and are still to this day) going to make a home in Louisville. We had just built a house there, which we were planning on living in half the time. Prior to my career ending, we obviously were living in Buffalo the other half of the year when I was working. Leslie's originally from Louisville. We met there. So, for this next chapter of our lives, I wanted to honor her by living in Louisville, where she could be around her family. My family is pretty close in Cincinnati, which worked out great for both of us.

So that was number one on the non-negotiable list.

Number two was I didn't (and still don't) want to take a job or pursue anything that went outside of my core values. So, my next job can't put me in situations that would compromise my health, my faith, or my marriage.

Then the third was I didn't want to risk our current lifestyle by high-stakes investing or some other kind of high-risk venture. I had worked hard to build this lifestyle for us so we could live comfortably for a long time. It doesn't mean I don't have dreams of being at the next level of wealth and being more generous or more impactful with our money and resources. But I didn't ever want to risk what we have to pursue what's next.

Once You Have Your Core Values, Write Them Down

Your core values evolve and shift over the years, and that's perfectly normal. One of the great things about growing older is after a while, you start to see things a little differently, a little more clearly. For me, my value system has changed slightly over the years. I think ever since I left football, my values have become even more intentional. I don't want to do anything that violates my value system.

I have these core values written in visible places in my house. I have one list of them on a whiteboard opposite of where I do my remote podcasts, so I can just glance up and look at them if I ever need a reminder. Everyone's values are a little different, and that's okay. Here are mine.

Eric's Core Values

1. Loyalty to God, family, and friends

2. Great discipline and work ethic

3. Being generous

4. Having fun and a positive attitude in life

5. Prioritizing my health

The first one, loyalty to God, family, and friends, is a no-brainer for me. I'm not going to do stuff that compromises my relationship with them. I want to be loyal and express my appreciation for them. You show loyalty by committing time to be in their presence. Trying to be the best version of yourself for them. Never speaking badly about them, and learning as much as you can about them so you can be there for them.

Number two is great discipline and work ethic, because great things follow discipline in life. I'm just passionate about being disciplined in life, which always will bear fruit. No matter what, you'll prepare yourself for those big opportunities if you have and practice personal discipline. When they come, you will be happy with the person in the mirror. If self-confidence comes from keeping the promises you've made to yourself, then are you doing on a daily basis what you have committed to? Keeping promises to yourself can only come with tremendous self-discipline.

Work ethic is part of the same core value. There's a direct relationship between being disciplined and having unstoppable drive. I want to be all-in on everything I'm doing. I have an obsessive personality, and I believe that is fine as long as I'm channeling that obsession to positive things in my life.

Number three is being generous. I've been blessed with generational wealth, and I feel it is important to be generous to the people and causes I feel are important. But even if I hadn't the same kind of financial resources, I would have the same core value. Being generous is a state of mind, and not necessarily about giving away wealth. You can be generous with your time, your efforts, or sharing what you do have with people who will appreciate it. Serving others is a form of generosity. My kids exercise their generosity every week when they run our neighbor's trash bins in from the curb—it gives them great joy. Generosity gives me great joy, too.

Number four is having fun in life. I sometimes think when you are a high achiever or high performer, it feels like it takes the pleasure out of life. Don't get me wrong—winning and succeeding is fun. But there's something to be said about just taking trips with the family and goofing around, and having some beers around a fire, telling stories, and cutting up on each other. Or golf trips to play incredible courses around the country. Or quick trips with Leslie to give her a break from the kids and time for us to focus on each other. To me, that adds the spice of life that makes all the hard work and discipline worth it. It also allows me to keep a positive attitude on those periods of life that require intense focus and discipline.

And then the last one is prioritizing my health, and that's for a few reasons. One, I just feel that ultimately, if you don't have your health, you don't have anything. You can't enjoy the fruits of your labor. You can't have an impact on others. I sacrificed my health in a lot of ways playing football.

It's up there with maybe one of the most physically demanding professions out there. Now, post-football, I prioritize taking the weight off, taking care of my body, staying in good shape so that I can spend time with my family. I want to pour my energy into them, like playing with my kids for as long as I possibly can.

And it's important to me to have my health to make an impact for Christ, and on the lives He puts on my path.

***

Writing your values down and seeing them often is a vital part of making them live through you. It's not that I don't know what my fundamental values are without the posted list—it's that I want a constant reminder of what I'm about, a sort of rigid boundary so it's no longer a question of what I will do or what I won't do.

After a while, these values just become you. There is a lot of power in choosing what your values are and standing by them. It takes a lot of guessing out of situations.

Back when I was playing for the Bills, they had their own set of values posted everywhere for the players to see them. Before that, for the longest time, we had no idea what our core values were with the Bills. But that changed. Suddenly, when you walked into our practice facility, the core values were stated there every single day—an acronym using the word *heart*:

- Hard work
- Energy
- Accountability
- Respect
- Team

Every day, our core values and the organization's core values were branded into our brains. We lived, ate, and breathed it. And it showed in how we treated each other as a team and how we approached the game. I'll never forget that.

Design Your Life and Schedule Based on Your Core Values

When you have a solid idea about who you are, many things in your life become crystal clear and are no longer a question.

Then you go one step further: you actively plan your life on your core values. I very much believe that you become your thoughts and behavior—so you have to be careful about your behavior on a day-to-day basis. You need to create a schedule that flows from that. It reflects who you are as a person. I fill up my schedule with things that I know will feed my soul, help make my body and mind healthier, get me closer to my family, and find the joy and fun in everyday life. Honestly, I don't have any room for anything else.

One of the things I do is fill my schedule with enough obligations that I'm actively pursuing Christ, whether it's a men's group or a couple's Bible study, or it's church on Sunday. I fight to fill my schedule with enough of the good stuff that weeds out some of the other riffraff.

Having fun in life is also one of my values, so there's some balance there, too. But even my idea of fun also fulfills some of my other core values. For example, if I'm going to play a game of golf,

I'm also exercising my body for health, loving nature and appreciating God's creation, and using great discipline to try and perfect my golf swing. (My golf swing is a long way from perfect.)

By filling your life with activities that fulfill your core values, the other things automatically fall off. You only have the capacity to internalize so much stuff. So, if you're internalizing a positive podcast, if you're reading self-development books or books with a positive message, if you are spending time with those close to you, you'll reap incredible benefits. You're going to be happier and feel more fulfilled.

You're also eliminating the negative self-talk. You're removing the people in your life who don't serve you, who bring you down or bring things into your life that negatively influence you. Being aligned with your core values just brings you closer to who you were meant to be and makes you a shining light. People may just want to be around you, and they may not even be sure why.

One of the men I admire who has a solid sense of his core values and living them to the fullest is Keith Craft. Keith is the lead pastor of Elevate Life Church, a non-denominational church in Frisco, Texas. He is also an influential leader, author, and speaker and has shared the stage with some of the best speakers in the world, including ex-presidents.

One of the things Keith said is, "Whatever you honor, you will attract. Whatever you dishonor, you will retract out of your life." I think that's such a powerful statement and couldn't be more accurate.

Having the Courage to Reach Out

Being firmly grounded in your core values gives you a certain freedom and confidence. When you robustly live your values, you start to get a better sense of other people who share your values, maybe even people you don't know. And conversely, they get a better understanding of the real you.

On my podcast, "What's Next With Eric Wood," I started with fellow football players as guests and professional athletes from other sports as well. I was learning and being inspired by other athletes and their processes, how they overcame obstacles and what made them tick. As time went by, I became interested in thought leaders and motivational speakers. A lot of these people changed my life and altered how I saw things. Suddenly my future and circle of influence got a lot bigger, just by having the courage to reach out and connect on my podcast.

I'll reach out via social media or try to find a mutual connection in some way, shape, or form to guys who inspire me—Ed Mylett and Steve Weatherford. Also, I love having on former teammates or athletes who I know have a great story or could be inspiring or fun.

My larger point is to exercise your courage to reach out to people who model the values you strive to live to. Use the tools at your disposal! You'd be surprised how many people would respond and be touched by your outreach. Social media is an incredible tool to express your values. Once you start putting it out there, you start to attract others with those same values. Finding people of like mind and similar values can help you go further and enrich each other.

I try to align myself with the people I admire and strive to be like. I want to elevate them because they've made an impact on my life, and I want to learn more. I want people to learn from them as well, let them affect their lives. It's incredible how much you can learn about someone in just an hour and how much you can take away from listening to others.

When you start doing a deep dig into someone else's life and ask, "Hey, if you could do this differently, what would you do?" Once you discover the treasure trove of someone's lifetime of learning, you can truly learn something new and get inspired.

Key Takeaways

Here are the key takeaways about core values:

- Examine your core values. Are you living up to them?
- If you don't know what your core values are, do the work to find them.
- Seek others who model the core values that you want.
- Define your hard boundaries.
- Once you have your core values, write them down.
- Design your life and schedule based on your core values.
- Have the courage to reach out.

6 Focus On Your Health

If you don't take time for your wellness, you will be forced to take time for your illness.

—Joyce Sunada

You are lucky enough to be put on this earth for a reason.

Your time here is precious, and the quality of that time is directly related to how much you take care of yourself. If you can't take care of yourself and thrive, you will leave the planet too early, and you will rob the rest of the world of all the gifts you have to offer.

Starting from that perspective, you might begin to look at your health a little differently. It's not just about you. It's about everyone who might benefit from interacting with you from now until your last days. Without my long-term health, I don't feel like I can live to the full potential that God has intended for me through the gifts he's given me.

I'm always trying to be an example for those around me—especially for my family—so I'm constantly trying to model healthy habits for them. Along the same lines, I believe that the best leaders show steadily the example of what they are preaching, so I always want to be a healthy example to those I'm looking to lead. No one wants to take advice from someone who looks like they just ate a box of doughnuts before they walked in (a line my performance coach buddy, Ben Newman, and I will often say to each other). It simply would indicate that there is likely a lack of discipline often in certain areas of that person's life, healthy eating being one of them.

I have always felt that it's been easier for me to follow individuals who have tremendous discipline in their life, and a healthy physique usually is the first sign of that on meeting them. Sean McDermott, the current coach of the Buffalo Bills (whom you heard from in the foreword), wakes up at 4 am to ensure he gets his daily workout in and abides by a healthy eating structure. When he stands in front of the team to talk about discipline, that goes a lot further than from those who do not commit to a healthy lifestyle.

Your Unique Health Focus Requires Vision and Perspective

If you are at your pivot point, then focusing on your health is critical. Now, more than ever, you are relying on your body and mind to make big moves. There is a reason I started this book with examining your gifts, choosing a greater perspective, having a vision, and examining your core values—you need a strong foundation in those basics so you know *why* you are focusing on your health. Your health journey is personal and about you, yet it is also about your vision and positively influencing everyone you touch along the way.

Everyone's health journey is unique. You should tailor your regimen to your goals and the things that are most important to you. I talk about my training not because I want you to mimic it—that's not my intention. It's to pull back the curtains on why I trained the way I did, how I approached my health at that time because of the specific vision I had. As my vision changed, so did the way I approached my health.

Also, I want to emphasize that if you plan to change your diet or adopt a new fitness regimen, please consult with your doctor. My choices are my own and not necessarily suitable for everyone else.

And I also want to add that everybody's body is different, so use your common sense and instinct to determine what may be right for you.

Early Health Sacrifices in My Football Career

Before being in the NFL, starting in high school, I realized that I was going to have to do some extreme things to my body—things that, from a longevity standpoint, might not be the best. So I understood I was making sacrifices for the short and maybe not-so-short term.

I felt it was going to be worth it for me. That started with my junior year of high school when I quit playing basketball for my high school team and primarily just lifted weights six days a week. I started by gaining 55 pounds my junior year of high school, and I gained another 45 pounds my senior year. The following year heading into the University of Louisville, I showed up weighing 300 pounds. Between 18 and 24 months, putting on a hundred pounds was significant—but it was something that I had to do.

No, that's not great for your body, but it enabled me to get my *one* scholarship to college.

In college, I started 49 straight games and never missed a game with an injury. Of course, you get dinged up along the way, and you play through some things, but that's the sacrifice you make with the game of football. And there are many reasons why you'd make that sacrifice, especially as an offensive lineman because you never want to let the guys down on your offensive line. I couldn't have withstood the constant pounding if I didn't commit to putting on all of those pounds.

Going into the NFL and maintaining a weight between 305 and 310 was tough. It was an enormous number of calories. So I would wake up in the morning and immediately start pounding food or shakes until bedtime. Every day ended with some type of food or another shake, just to keep the weight on.

I realized some of the costs at the time. There were injuries and surely some traumatic brain injury along the way with all of the hits, but I always say there are inherent risks in any profession. My mom dealt cards for a living at a casino, and she ended up getting carpal tunnel syndrome in both wrists. There's going to be some physical harm with any profession that requires repetitive movements—even if you're only sitting at a desk and typing on a keyboard.

There were many reasons why I was willing to take on those health risks. The ability to live out the dream of playing in the NFL, the relationships, the rush of playing the game you love in front of huge crowds, to use the gifts God has given me, and to create generational wealth for my family and also to be generous to those in need are all reasons why I would make those health sacrifices.

Now, football is an extreme vocation of oftentimes brutal combat, but that's not a lifetime of work. Instead, it was a temporary sacrifice to pursue something I loved in order to achieve high success.

After Football: Getting My Long-Term Health Back on Track

After my final football injury, there was a lot to reassess. I had to make a new plan to take care of myself from then on. My years in the NFL had not been kind to my body, even though I felt I had a healthy perspective about all the injuries I had sustained. But on paper, it looked intimidating. I had six lower-body surgeries while I was playing. When your NFL career ends, you get a disability checkup from an independent doctor that the NFL and the NFL Players Association picks.

When I went there, the independent doctor gave me 27 different x-rays to determine what was maybe going to ail me moving forward—injuries that could possibly inhibit me from certain types of work. So, with his guidance, along with other health experts, I needed to lose some weight. I also had to start training differently so I wasn't pounding my body nearly as much. I had my neck injury, but that didn't require immediate surgery; it required some rehab and treatment. From that point on, I needed to pay attention and avoid certain activities. I still have disc and bone sitting at a very dangerous spot near my spinal cord.

But first and foremost, I needed to lose weight. There were a lot of habits I had built up ever since I was 16 years old, ever since I had started trying to put on weight for football. So I had to start avoiding the pantry for the first time in 16 years.

I have to admit it felt pretty weird.

Developing New Habits

One of my favorite new habits I've adopted is intermittent fasting, which means choosing an eating regimen in which you switch between your regular healthy meals and not eating at all. Fasting has a weird stigma in our American culture. It's still seen as an unusual practice, something not really in the mainstream. But it's funny because nearly every other culture worldwide uses fasting for health or religious purposes. Fasting has been around for thousands of years, since biblical times.

Part of the reason I like intermittent fasting is that it puts time restraints on when I can eat. It also offers a lot of health benefits. By restricting my eating window each day, I can still eat to be full and then continue to lose weight. You also feel a small win each day when you complete your 12- to 18-hour fast for abiding to that discipline. And so, my workouts changed—everything changed, but I was able to lose weight and make some progress.

That competitive part of my nature, one of my most important gifts, has been such an asset when getting back into shape and working on my new habits. Now, if there's not some type of competition, if there's not something I'm working toward, it's hard for me to find motivation. For instance, this year, I ended up running a half marathon. Part of the training challenge was to run 100 miles in eight weeks, which isn't a crazy amount when you break it down to day-to-day.

But for me, I had never done distance running in my life. So, it was a total changeup, which was kind of exciting. Instead of just running, I was doing a different type of workout—more high-intensity interval training instead of straight power training and endurance for the field training. You could call them boot camp–style classes. I paired this with a reasonably low-carbohydrate diet and started getting steady results.

I own part of a gym in Louisville. So, I just started going to the classes with everybody else. I would generally hit the 9 am class, which was when many moms who had just dropped their kids off at school would come to work out. So, it was the housewives and me for a few months. And it's funny; I may have appeared unapproachable because people just assume that I would be doing my football-style workouts. But really I want to work out like a normal, functioning, healthy member of society. I'm no longer training for hand-to-hand combat in the trenches!

Dealing with Traumatic Brain Injury

One of the significant issues that I knew I had to deal with was the long-term impacts of traumatic brain injury (often referred to as TBI). It's become a big issue with NFL players nowadays. Many are concerned about brain injuries, and with good reason because of all the constant hits to the head. Doctors are seeing serious ramifications from former players starting in their 60s and sometimes younger than that now.

Having played center for nine years in the NFL where I had contact on every play, obviously, this is a concern of mine now.

But when you're playing, you put it on the backburner. It's not something you can think about when you're up there—if you do, you're just not going to be able to play at your full potential. So I knew that it was time to address any issues I might be facing and develop an assessment and plan.

I was lucky to get connected with Dr. Daniel Amen, who is a psychiatrist and brain disorder specialist and a prominent media figure in his own right.

I went to his clinic and got a full assessment, which included a series of brain scans. I committed to a six-month rehabilitation program, which involved spending time in a hyperbaric oxygen chamber, daily sauna sessions, some different supplements, and dietary recommendations. I had terrible blood flow in the areas of my brain affected by TBI. With the new rehab program in place, the goal was to heal the brain and improve blood flow.

A lot of people don't know that you can actively heal the brain and that the brain is capable of neurogenesis, literally growing new brain neurons and nerve cells, for your entire life. Sure enough, in a little over six months, they were able to find significant improvements in my brain scans. Blood flow has dramatically improved to certain parts of my brain that I had damaged when playing football all those years.

You are never "done" with taking care of your brain, so there are specific ways of eating and recovering that I will be practicing for the long term.

The Three Pillars of Recovery

As a professional athlete, I thought about recovery quite a bit, because it is an essential part of being ready to play on the field. When I was playing football, it seemed like it was *all* about recovery, getting prepared to perform the next day, and there was no option of missing it.

So, I always had to recover to perform the next day. If you had a terrible night of sleep the night before the game, nobody cared. You figure out pretty quickly that getting good rest and recovery time is the player's responsibility. No matter what happens the next day, you're going to be held accountable for your performance on the field.

I had to ensure I was getting good sleep, training in a way that supported my energy, rehydrating appropriately, and getting the proper nutrition. We had coaches and other people who would instruct us on all those things. At the end of the day, though, it was on you as a player to get yourself ready.

Another way to think about recovery is recharging. Just like your phone, you are multitasking all day, feeling like you are moving at 1,000 miles an hour and dealing with a lot of information and tasks. Just like that phone, you get depleted and need to recharge. Everyone needs periods of recovery to operate at an optimal level, not just athletes.

Over time, I've learned that there are three pillars to complete an effective recovery: sleep, nutrition, and movement.

The First Pillar: Sleep

When you are in a big transition in life, you need to approach every day as game-ready and have a regimen of recovery built into your lifestyle. Whether you're trying to be positive around the house, or be a patient parent and spouse, whether you're a businessperson, whatever it is, you need the energy from the recovery to perform each day. It's so easy to slip on the first pillar and not get enough sleep. I know I fall into this trap as well. If I just cheat myself out of an hour of sleep, I'll inevitably feel it at some point during the day. I'll be drained, moody, and not nearly as productive.

It's tough because, in our work culture, it seems to be a badge of honor nowadays to go without sufficient sleep. How often have you heard, "I only got four hours of sleep last night! I'm getting so much done." Ultimately, that is going to haunt you. There is so much data out there on the importance of high-quality sleep and recovery for your productivity, mood, concentration, and general creativity.

Athletes know the importance of sleep and restoration all too well. For me, it has become imperative because of my past traumatic brain injury. Now that we know that neurogenesis can promote healing and new development in the brain until the day we die, then high-quality sleep becomes a necessity. Most neurogenesis happens during deep sleep—so I need to prioritize that to make sure that I can perform and be cognitively sound.

Recent research indicates about 1% of the population can perform well on less than six hours of sleep a night. Those rare people have those genes, but for most of us, we need more.

On the opposite end of the spectrum, some people need even more, and that's okay.

LeBron James sleeps nine hours a night; J. J. Watt sleeps nine hours a night, too. So many high performers make sure they get the rest they need by prioritizing their sleep.

I realize we're not all perfect—inevitably, you're going to have a night that you didn't get enough sleep. Parents especially know this to be true! But the more we can make getting good sleep the rule rather than the exception, the better we're going to feel all around.

The Second Pillar: Nutrition

Even through high school, I had a basic idea that all calories were great and were created equal, whether they came from vegetables or ice cream. Throughout college, I started to shift a little bit toward being nutritionally conscious. This shift started at the time when I came down with mono, and I had to miss spring football.

Since initially bulking up in high school, any time I'd ever been hurt or sick, I would drop weight like crazy because I needed constant calories. I also needed to be lifting to keep the weight on, so I lost about 30 pounds when I got mono. I got down to about 270. One of our assistant strength coaches at the time was a guy named Kurt Schmidt (now at the University of Tennessee). He would take me grocery shopping and show me how on a budget I could get excellent nutritional fuel to build the weight back on the healthy way.

That guidance from Kurt was a blessing. He helped me strip a lot of the junk weight that I had packed on over the past year to prepare for football. It's impossible to put on 100 pounds of good weight in a year and a half to two years, so it stripped a lot of that fat off, and I was able to put back on more muscle by building it the right way with a better nutrition program. Since then, I became devoted to nutrition because I saw a difference. I got stronger, faster, and I was able to put on more muscle. I could move better because I had a better body composition.

When it comes to precisely the right nutritional program for your body, it can vary wildly depending on your health goals. And on top of that, everyone's body is different. So it's really up to you to research and find the right thing for you. I can only tell you what worked for me, and even then, there was a lot of trial and error before I found the right balance.

Nowadays, good nutrition is a huge part of my philosophy and that keeps me in the weight range that I find acceptable. Now, I live by the 80% to 90% rule, meaning 80% or 90% of the time, I have strict guidelines for nutrition and fasting. For fasting, that's usually a 12-hour or 18-hour fasting window, depending on how active I am. Also, 80% to 90% of the time, I eat lean protein, veggies, healthy fats, and some berries. The focus for me is real food and not processed or packaged as much as possible. That is what most of my diet consists of. We eat as organic as we can with the produce and grass-fed, cage-free with the meats.

If we do splurge on the weekend, maybe a bit in excess of not-so-healthy foods and drinks, I know we can reset and get back on track. Anytime we do that, my wife and I will generally fast from dinner Sunday night to dinner Monday night. And generally, by Tuesday morning, all the inflammation is gone, and we're back to square one.

I read a fascinating book called *Genius Foods* by Max Lugavere about eating the right kinds of foods to help you "become smarter, happier, and more productive while protecting your brain for life."

Lugavere started on his health journey after his mother had an early onset of dementia. Using his media credentials and skills as a journalist, he spent years pouring over medical research and contacting some of the best minds in the field. He concluded that there was a lot to be discovered about nutrition that wasn't in the mainstream. He lists many of the foods that are healthy for your brain, such as lean proteins, almonds, avocados, extra virgin olive oil, leafy greens—foods that many health gurus have trumpeted for years—but Lugavere goes into the science of why they're so good for the brain.

Genius Foods inspired me, and his research helped guide me into the kinds of foods that I like to keep in the house. To my kids, I explain them as "brain foods" and "beast foods." Lean proteins are the beast foods in our house, the significant protein sources that help our bodies perform. Then we have our brain foods, like blueberries, leafy greens, avocados, and everything else Lugavere mentions in his book.

When your kids see you enjoy eating healthy food, they just love it. My son sees me make a big deal about salmon, and he sees how much I like it. And I don't say, "I have to eat this." I say, "Man, how lucky am I to eat my favorite meal any day I like?" When I take Gracie on one of our daddy/daughter dates to sushi, I know she likes it. And I think part of why she likes it is because she knows I love it.

Bottom line—you have to make an effort to eat healthily and put the proper nutrition in your body. But, if you make it part of your lifestyle, it won't feel like a sacrifice. The more you start eating healthy foods, the better you will feel, and the more healthy foods you will crave. The more you model healthy eating, the easier and more natural it will come for your kids. And that way, if you eat healthy 80% to 90% of the time, then cheating a little with the occasional junk food won't be a disaster.

The Third Pillar: Movement (aka Exercise)

I call the third pillar *movement*, but some might call it *exercise* instead. I've been athletically moving my whole life, ever since my childhood, so exercising comes as second nature to me. It's just in my DNA. If you find yourself in a sedentary lifestyle with not much history or experience with exercising, it's never too late to start. The trick is just to begin and stick with it.

It's kind of funny that the cure for a tired and out-of-shape body is to move it more, but there it is. Unlike machines, our bodies get stronger and more able the more we use them, even into old age. Provided we are getting enough sleep and fueling it with the proper nutrition, there's very little that can stop us if we keep a regular exercise regimen. Movement and exercise are a form of recovery.

On top of that, exercise helps our emotional and mental states, as well. It benefits the whole person, and once you get into the regular practice of it, you'll never want to quit. You're just going to feel way better than when you don't exercise.

On the flip side, the remedy for too much movement, such as a sore body or weakness from strenuous exercise, is also movement. Whenever my teammates and I would finish a game, the next day, we would all be incredibly sore in one way or the other. That sore feeling comes from a significant buildup of lactic acid in your body, which is a substance produced by your muscles when they exert themselves. (Also, from a whole bunch of collisions during the game.)

Instinctively, it may feel counterintuitive to keep moving your body when it hurts, but to get the lactic acid out of your system naturally, that's precisely what you need to do. You need to move, stretch, walk around, or even lift weights. This is what we call *active recovery*. Resting, by itself, will take you longer to relieve the symptoms of soreness and fatigue.

Active recovery is something I learned a lot about during my college and NFL career. The day after the game, we would come into the facility, and we would get moving. We would get a lift in or run around. We had to get moving to recover. We wouldn't work strenuously to the point of exhaustion or injury—you don't want to pile on. But we had to get our bodies moving for the lactic acid to flush itself naturally.

We had to be in touch with our bodies and know what we could and couldn't do. So, we started with cardiovascular work. For example, if you were capable, you would run. If you couldn't run at top speed, you might run 10 sprints at a 75% pace. If you couldn't run at all, you could hop on a bike. If you couldn't bike, you could get into an underwater treadmill. This machine was a partially submerged treadmill that takes a lot of the load off of your lower body. Basically, the routine was to move in some way, shape, or form. Just to get the blood flowing again throughout your body.

In general, we found the right combination of stretching, cardiovascular, and strength exercises to soothe the symptoms of soreness while also maintaining our strength and helping our bodies through active recovery. I believe movement is a critical part of the solution for all lifestyles.

If you find yourself having trouble staying consistent, revisit your vision and core values. What are you here on earth to achieve? What kind of exercise would best serve your longevity, stamina, goals, and overall health? How can your body best serve your potential?

Remember the people who will be potentially affected by your positive influence over a lifetime. Your health serves a higher purpose.

One of my favorite Bible verses talks about the importance of maintaining your health. It's from 1 Corinthians 6:19–20:

Do you not know that your bodies are temples of the Holy Spirit, who is in you, whom you have received from God? You are not your own; you were bought at a price. Therefore honor God with your bodies.

As a man of deep faith, I take that particular verse to heart. God has put me here and has special plans for me. Who am I to abuse the gift of this body? I must do everything in my power to maintain, improve, and cherish it.

I believe everyone can create an active lifestyle that will enhance and protect their health, no matter what age and even if they feel they have limited athletic ability. It doesn't matter. During the pandemic, many people took up brisk walking or running just to get out of the house. Just a 15-minute walk has tremendous health benefits for the body and brain. Everyone has a different exercise style, so if you're not sure, try some things out. Whether it's walking, swimming, yoga, a team sport, hiking, weight training . . . there are virtually unlimited ways to exercise your body. The key is just to start.

You've got one body to use as your tool for engaging the world with your gifts. Remember to treat it with love, care, and respect.

Key Takeaways

Here are the key takeaways about focusing on your health:

- You are here for a reason, and your health serves a higher purpose.

- The quality of your time on earth is directly related to how well you take care of your health.

- Every health journey is unique.

- Your unique health focus requires vision and perspective.

- If you're out of practice with your health, you can always get back on track.

- It's never too late to develop new habits.

- Be mindful of your brain health.

- Recovery is essential for all lifestyles.

- There are three pillars to recovery and health: sleep, nutrition, and movement.

- Maintain an active lifestyle that works for you.

- Remember to treat your body with love, care, and respect.

7 Get into a Routine That Sets You Up for Success

Simple daily disciplines—little productive action, repeated consistently over time—add up to the difference between failure and success.

—Jeff Olson

What if the secret to your success was small and simple?

You are creating your future by the things you do every day. So every little thing is significant. And that's why starting with a morning and daily routine to set you up for success is vital in the long run.

Your morning routine is where the rubber hits the road. If you have a particular vision about what you want from life, how are you putting that into practice today and every day? If you have a solid idea about your core values, how are you putting those values into action? If you are focusing on your health, what are you doing every day to move your health forward?

The truth is you already have a morning routine. Most of the time, you do the same things every morning and then later into the day. So the question then becomes—is your routine intentional? Is it supporting your future? Or is your routine just something that you do every day without really thinking about it?

The things you do at the beginning of the day can help you seize control of your life and get intentional about the future. Even the seemingly most minor things can make the most significant difference over time. William H. McRaven, a retired US Navy four-star admiral, gave a famous college commencement speech about the importance of the little things. For him, it all started with making the bed. McRaven said:

It was a simple task, mundane at best. But every morning, we were required to make our bed to perfection. It seemed a little ridiculous at the time, particularly in light of the fact that we were aspiring to be real warriors, tough battle-hardened SEALs, but the wisdom of this simple act has been proven to me many times over.

If you make your bed every morning, you will have accomplished the first task of the day. It will give you a small sense of pride, and it will encourage you to do another task and another and another. By the end of the day, that one task completed will have turned into many tasks completed. Making your bed will also reinforce the fact that little things in life matter. If you can't do the little things right, you will never do the big things right. (*UT News*)

Those "little things" that McRaven refers to are all the actions and micro-actions that add up to the totality of your day. Those days turn into weeks and those weeks into months and years. The little things have a cumulative effect over time, adding up to an enormous benefit.

Jeff Olson wrote a great book called *The Slight Edge*, which explains that the secret to your success is in the daily activities of your life. With study after study, he proves that little actions, compounded over time, reap incredible results:

> The truth is, what you do matters. What you do today matters. What you do every day matters. Successful people just do the things that seem to make no difference in the act of doing them and they do them over and over and over until the compound effect kicks in. (p. 58)

If everything little thing you do matters . . . what are you doing? That may be one of the most critical questions of your life.

Most people are not intentional about their mornings. I'll start with a fairly basic example. You may begin with an alarm going off, followed by immediately checking the phone for any texts, emails, notifications, or news alerts. Then, you might get ready for the day through a typical morning shower and hygiene, followed by breakfast and a commute to work. While on your commute, you might listen to some music, news, or one of the morning shows. Then, you're probably on autopilot for the rest of the day—commute home, make dinner, maybe squeeze some exercise in, watch some TV, and go to bed.

That routine is not a recipe for disaster, but it also isn't very intentional and won't move you forward. Chances are if you stick with that routine, whatever you are experiencing now, you're just going to get more of the same. Some people are happy staying where they are and not advancing. But if you want to break out of that, and help fulfill the future you've set for yourself, then you've got to switch it up and get intentional.

It all starts with what you do in the morning, which leads you into the rest of the day.

The Built-In Routine of the NFL

I didn't think consciously about the importance of the daily routine until after I had left football. I didn't have to because my built-in routine was decided for me by the Bills' intense daily regimen. It was in all the training and learning I had to do to maintain my field-ready status even when we weren't playing. When you're a professional athlete, almost every minute of every day is accounted for. So I dedicated nearly all of my waking hours to football—it was part of my daily purpose.

During the season, my days were packed. I'd wake up early, usually before 6 am, get in my morning devotional or Bible reading, and then drive to the stadium for a workout first thing in the morning. Then I'd grab breakfast, take a shower, rehab any injuries in the training room, and be ready for football meetings to start at 8 am. Meetings would run from 8 to 11:30 am, and then we'd take a light meal and prep for practice. After that, we would practice for two to three hours. Then I'd shower, lunch, and potentially work out if I didn't knock one out in the morning. After that, it was back to meetings for two more hours.

The meetings required a lot of focus and energy and sometimes could run long. We would often have a film session in which we would study the opponents we were about to face by looking at footage of their performance on the field. Sometimes we would go over our performance to spot check things we could improve. We'd also study the depth chart, which is the placement of starting players and secondary players. Additionally, we'd focus heavily on the assignments—which are essentially how we're going to construct our plays to block the defense. Or, if you're a defensive player, you would study how to defeat the offensive scheme.

Then, I'd have time to get my treatment, which is essentially rehab for any physical issue that I needed to work on. It might be a cold tub, a sauna, or stretching. Sometimes we had an additional film session after that; that's when we would go over game footage at the end of the day. Between 4:30 and 6 pm, we would go home to our families, recover from all the activity, and start the whole thing over in the morning.

Throughout the entire daily and weekly routine, a whole team of people constantly evaluated us and gave feedback every step of the way. If I asked the question, "How am I doing?" I would get a precise answer and a metric that I could use to improve.

My mindset and optimism had to be on point because I was getting critiqued every day. I thrived on it and became addicted to constant feedback, because with continuous feedback, I could constantly improve. That was the mindset we all had to get into to be successful players.

We would all put our egos in check and focus on our performance. We were bringing it to the table every week, and we were craving to get better because it helped us keep our jobs and make more money. Steady improvement made us more successful and helped us leave a legacy behind that we could be proud of. So, we wanted to upgrade and advance, and we were highly responsive to the coaching because we had faith in our coaches to help us improve. The coaches earned respect through their work ethic and daily consistency, just like we did.

The Bills were clear about their vision—they wanted to win and take us to the top. We would be the best players to contribute to the team's success; the Bills just drilled that into us. So every day was a reflection of that vision—hundreds of small actions that added up to a formidable and cohesive team ready to play professional football at the top of our game.

The Struggle of Finding a New Routine

My post-football way of life was terribly disoriented at first. For the first time in my life, I didn't wake up each day needing to prepare for a workout. I didn't need to eat a certain way to stay 310 pounds. But, of course, I still held on to the structure around Leslie and our kids. I was still exercising my faith and doing some kind of morning devotional. But other than those things, I felt like I was adrift.

So, I just floated by. Days became weeks, and for the first time in my life, I started to suffer from anxiety. Lacking an explicit purpose was making me anxious, and there was no relief on the horizon. I didn't know what career path I was heading down. It didn't even need to be a career—I just needed to pursue something bigger than myself actively.

You don't have to be an athlete to empathize with difficulty coping from a lack of structure. Recently, many people were thrust into an unfamiliar routine during the pandemic—they had either too little or too much time on their hands. Neither is good for you. And I think that's a struggle for many people, especially when the situation forces them to be home when they have been used to going to the office or a job where everything is structured. Now, you supposedly have all this free time, but when are you able to be productive?

High Performers Have Similar Routines for Success

There had to be a way forward, I thought. I still worked with my executive coach, Mac, and was in the habit of listening to podcasts of people whom I admired. I also read a wide selection of self-development books that I thought would help bring me out of the funk I was experiencing. I was surprised to realize that the people I looked up to, all incredibly distinct from each other, had specific morning routines that set them up for success during their day.

I knew I was onto something, so I researched the different morning routines to see if I could find some common denominator. Interestingly, they found remarkably similar morning routines that helped lay the foundation for their short-term and long-term success. It should be no surprise that healthy, self-actualized people who are high performers often come to the same conclusions independently.

Almost all of the highly effective people I admired had some kind of gratitude practice. Some people write down the things they are grateful for, speak them aloud, or record them on a device. The point of it is to actively recognize the things you are grateful for in life. The results are phenomenal, as I'll explain in a moment.

The second common denominator was morning reading. For some people, that could be a biblical verse, self-development material, or some kind of nonfiction where you are learning something new. It's a way of feeding the mind with positive content to give a significant boost.

The third commonality was an extended moment of silence of some type. Meditation was a common choice in this area, which I highly recommend. It could also be breathing exercises or simple silent reflection. It could be dedicated time to yourself away from all digital devices and media content. It could be time simply in silent prayer. All of these activities have measurable benefits in the long term, and it's incredibly healthy to quiet the mind and free yourself from toxic distractions. The silence does wonders.

A morning ritual they almost all had in common, too, was some kind of workout. Some people start with a swim or a run, and others might prefer lifting, yoga, or tai-chi. Anything that gets your blood pumping and helps you get in touch with your body is excellent and has a tremendous positive long-term impact.

The combination of gratitude, morning reading, working out, and silent reflection helps people take control of the morning and start the day on their terms. They don't start in a frantic state, reacting to all the stimuli thrown at them as soon as they open their eyes. They don't let their phones or other devices bully them around and force them into a place of fear or anxiety. Instead, they feed their minds and souls calmly and intentionally, helping to prepare themselves for the day ahead.

The intentional routine also stimulates their creative juices, spawning new ideas and new ways to approach a problem that may need solving. And there was a bonus—a new routine helped me put structure around all the other things I needed to do to focus on my health.

Once I had my vision sorted out and a solid personal mission statement, I felt ready to shake things up and try new things in my morning routine that would eventually become a daily practice. That competitive streak in me popped up again, and I knew I could do a lot better than stumbling through my mornings lost, looking for something to do.

The New Routine That Works for Me

My morning routine is a constant work-in-progress, and at the same time, I'm thrilled with the one I have—it's producing great results.

I encourage you to experiment and formulate what works for you. However, I feel strongly that you must have some form of gratitude, silence, reading, and physical activity to have the most impact on your life. After that, it's all customization.

When I wake up in the morning, it's completely device-free. I've banned the phone or other devices from the bedroom. I bought a separate alarm clock to wake me up. It's extremely freeing, not waking up in a reactive state. Once you pick up your phone, you're looking at messages, you're reading emails and news, and your whole state of mind gets hijacked.

Next, I pour myself a special hydration drink. It doesn't taste the greatest, but it's great for hydration, digestion, controlling my blood sugar, and mental alertness. It also has fantastic anti-inflammatory properties. I wanted to share the recipe with you in case you'd like to try it.

Eric Wood's Awesome Morning Drink

- 40 oz alkaline water
- 2 tbl of apple cider vinegar
- 1 tbl lemon juice
- 1 tsp turmeric
- 1 tsp Ceylon cinnamon
- 1 tsp cayenne pepper
- 2 pinches of pink Himalayan salt
- one serving of creatine and beta-alanine

Next, I'll go to my office for some kind of journaling. Sometimes it's a gratitude journal, where I write three unique things that I am grateful for. Lately, I've been working with Ben Greenfield's spiritual disciplines journal, which also includes gratitude. It's got a little bit of scripture reading, and I'll read a morning devotional that takes me about 10 minutes. For me, I look at it as similar to tithing, which is giving 10% back to God. Well, I like to give God at least the first 10 minutes of my productive time of the day. That's another win that aligns me with who I want to be in life.

I recently received a pro tip from one of my buddies, David Nurse, who recommended writing a daily journal entry to Leslie every day for a year. These were often short recaps of the day before or something the kids said or did that brought us joy or laughter. These entries would often involve just an affirmation about her as well. I did it from one birthday of hers to the next. That journal traveled all around the country with me and was even left in Florida once and had to be mailed back! It was an additional daily commitment, but I am so glad that I completed it. I may have cried harder than her when I gave it to her, but she was definitely blown away by it.

I like to involve a little prayer practice or quiet time after the devotional. Sometimes it's just silence, and sometimes it's active prayer. Sometimes I'll just sit there and take in my surroundings for a few minutes in the form of meditation. That's pretty much how I start every single day. No matter what's going on, I find a way to make it work. Clearing my mind and starting my day intentionally just works wonders for the rest of the day.

This quiet time also gives me an opportunity to formulate a short-term vision for the day. Who do I want to be this day? What good am I going to do in the next 12 to 16 hours? Who will I serve this day? That's a question in Ben Greenfield's spiritual disciplines journal that I love. Pondering that question puts me in the proper mindset for the day.

Another thing I do as part of my morning routine, which many people might find intense, is subjecting myself to some cold exposure. Many high performers have the same habit. If I don't feel refreshed entirely from the night before, I'll pop in a cold shower. It completely reinvigorates me.

More important, there's reliable research out there that cold exposure has neurological and physical benefits. Exposure to the cold activates the thermogenesis process, which can help you burn fat throughout the day. The extra benefit is that it wakes you up, and honestly, it knocks out a win first thing in the morning. I like that feeling that I did something that pushed me outside of my comfort zone. If I can deal with this uncomfortable thing first thing in the morning, I can deal with other uncomfortable things that come up during the rest of the day.

I work out at some point of the day. Usually, it's right before or after my reading or quiet time. Regardless, I want to get in at least a good 30 minutes before I have to start my day with broadcasting or podcasting or other work. So I don't even touch my phone until I finish my morning routine.

Intentionality: You Get to Decide How Your Day Will Go

As I mentioned, your morning routine is so important because you are starting the day intentionally and not just waking up and flying by the seat of your pants. Certainly, things can happen throughout the day that you don't expect and have no control over. However, you can have much more control of everything if you take the time to decide how you will react, what you will do, and who you will be at the beginning of the day. Leave your phone out of it—this time is yours!

You get to decide early how great your day is going to be. You can design your day and be in control. That intentionality gives you the tool to say, "This is the day I want. Here are the things I want to do." It prepares you for whatever comes next and gets you field ready for anything that might pop up. Of course, all kinds of different (and sometimes difficult) things can happen to you during the day. But if you hold your intention, your odds are much higher to stay true to your purpose than if you start your morning saying, "Well, whatever. Let's see what happens."

For me, my quiet time enables me to be more present and intentional with my family. When I do see them, because of my personal mission statement, I want to have an impact on them. I want to be there for them, and it's a great time to remind myself of that. It's a great time to get reacquainted with yourself and revisit your vision, mission, core values, and ideal standards. What you're doing is building systems that reflect who you are at your deepest level.

Gratitude Changes Everything

The benefits of living with gratitude and gratitude practices are immeasurable. Studies have shown that when you spend 30 days writing three things you are grateful for each day, you can literally rewire your brain. In the 2012 *Psychology Today* article "The Grateful Brain," Alex Korb writes:

One study by a couple of American researchers assigned young adults to keep a daily journal of things they were grateful for (Emmons and McCullough, 2003). They assigned other groups to journal about things that annoyed them or reasons why they were better off than others. The young adults assigned to keep gratitude journals showed greater increases in determination, attention, enthusiasm, and energy compared to the other groups.

The same researchers went further and found that gratitude not only positively influenced the mind but it also affected the body in measurable ways. Korb went on:

Subjects assigned to journal weekly on gratitude showed greater improvements in optimism. That makes sense. But that's not all; it also influenced their behaviors. Keeping a gratitude journal also caused greater improvements in exercise patterns. Lastly, it also caused a reduction in physical ailments, so these subjects had fewer aches and pains.

When I work on my journaling in the morning, one of the first questions I ask myself is, "What are you grateful for?" So I'll write down three things that I'm grateful for. And it's fantastic; the more I practice gratitude, the more things I find to be grateful for, and the more I feel a sense of general well-being.

That's not unique to me—it's just part of how we are wired. Try it! It feels great, and you can start feeling the difference in your attitude immediately. Just start to look for things throughout your day for which you are grateful, which will make that practice as easy as possible. After that, things will just start popping out at you.

Some form of gratitude practice has been a part of my life even before I stopped playing football. I recognized early on how lucky I was to be playing in the NFL and took daily stock of it every day.

By the last year of the league, I had a favorite gratitude practice. I got the idea from author Jon Gordon, who does a "gratitude walk" every morning. I would do a gratitude drive on my way to the stadium. I would turn off all the sound in my car and focus on all the things I was grateful for. It was beautiful. I only lived about a mile from the stadium, but it was just enough time to reflect on all the wonderful things that had come into my life. I'd be driving before it was light out, and I'd see the stadium lights and think, "Man, how incredible is it that I get to go work at an NFL facility today? I only had one scholarship offered to a college that I was lucky to get. And then I was a first-round draft pick, and I got to stay with the same organization. And my job is not really in jeopardy today. And, I'm a captain of this team, and I get to represent this team that I love so much."

I would just fill myself with gratitude before I got there, and then my whole day would be different. It took a lot of the worry out of what could come that day about losing a rep in practice or whatever else I might have been worried about. I'd walk in with a little bounce in my step, and people probably thought I was goofing, but that routine helped set me up. What a vast difference, as opposed to just rolling out of bed, being a little groggy, and being in a reactive state—similar to waking up and letting your phone boss you around first thing in the morning.

Even on the days I was injured, when I would be driving with a boot on my leg because I had just come off surgery, I still felt grateful. I was saying to myself, "I can still walk. I get to go to work today." Gratitude also helps with being intentional and giving you that mindset to conquer that day. Even if the circumstances aren't ideal and they're not perfect, putting yourself in a "get to" mode and not a "have to" mode is valuable, because there are so many people who drive to work every day and say, "Man, I have to go to work again today. This stinks." But there are always people who would kill to have that job or are physically incapable of doing your job. So it all goes back to perspective coupled with gratitude. Do you appreciate what you have?

These days, I try to come up with three unique things each day to be grateful for, though I've had many repeats in the last few years. That's not a bad thing—it's good to remind yourself of what you are grateful for, even if you have mentioned it in the past.

Intentionality the Night Before Can Enhance Your Whole Next Day

As I became more advanced in my morning and daily routine, I started to work backward a little to set it up even more. For example, what could I do the night before my morning to make my next day even more manageable?

I became inspired, once again, by entrepreneur, coach, and author Craig Ballantyne. He wrote *Unstoppable* and influenced me in core values and all the non-negotiables I needed to set up in my life. I had the pleasure of hosting him on my podcast in Episode 86, "The World's Most-Disciplined Man."

Craig also wrote a book called *Perfect Day*, which heavily influenced my thinking about how my day should work. He comes at his morning from a slightly different perspective. Craig argues that most people have too many self-help routines in the morning before they get work done. You see, his dad was a farmer, and from his experience, it was always you knocked out your chores first thing in the morning. After that, you would get to your workout or whatever it may be. I don't necessarily follow that approach exactly, but it did get me thinking.

There are times when I need to be ultra-productive throughout the next day. What if, the night before, I could knock three chores out when the kids go down for bed? That will give me time to do my preferred morning routine and still have knocked out a few tasks prior. But ultimately, I need to get these things done. If I do those life maintenance things at night before my big day, then that's all the more room in my morning schedule to approach my day right.

It's a sort of like building on "how do I want my day to go?" If I can start "prepping my landing" for the next day the night before, then I'm just setting myself up for more success. Of course, I can ask myself the same question the night before, too. "How do I want my day to go tomorrow? And what are some little things I can do tonight to help make that a reality?" These activities can include everything from laying out your workout clothes to prepping breakfast and lunch. Every little thing counts!

Become a Super-Learner

I didn't invent my morning routine out of thin air. Instead, I adapted some things from my past, some practices from football and my faith, and a lot of new material. So much of it came from reading and consciously trying to learn as much as possible from successful people. That's one of the beautiful things about self-actualized and thriving people—they want to share their successful methods with others.

If you can put yourself into a super-learner mentality—absorbing anything and everything that might be helpful to you—then nothing can stop you. Read the self-development books that interest you. Listen to podcasts from people you admire and find inspirational. Watch videos that give you something positive and valuable to learn. Spend time with friends who uplift you and have positive practices you want to emulate. You don't have to go all in on any one technique. Instead, you can cherry-pick from here and there and put all kinds of different tools in your utility belt.

My podcast became a platform and an advanced learning curriculum for me. I was so curious about what makes different successful people tick and learning all these incredible techniques that work. It gave me lots of new ideas and a free license to experiment with other methods. The great thing is if you are at a pivot point and having a rough time, what do you have to lose by trying something new?

I talk to about 40 or 50 high performers a year on my podcast. I found many common "Denominators" for successful routines. Yet, I didn't implement everything.

After absorbing everything you can, ultimately, it's up to *you* to find the best routine for your life, core values, and vision. Be intentional, learn from the best, and borrow what works.

Habit Stacking

As you experiment with your daily routine, you'll start to find the things that work for you and that you can do every day. One advanced technique I like to use to solidify a new habit is "habit stacking."

My good friend Kyle Idleman has a lot to say on the topic. He is a bestselling author and teaching pastor at Southeast Christian Church in Louisville, one of the largest churches in America. He is an incredible soul, and I am lucky to have such a great friend in my life. He introduced me to habit stacking years ago, and we talked about it in Episode 61 of my podcast, "The Value of Connection." Kyle learned about the practice from the book *Habit Stacking* by S. J. Scott.

Habit stacking is a way of associating a new habit with an old one. This association makes it easier and faster for your brain to solidify the habit, pairing new neural connections with stronger, older, and more established ones. For example, I like to memorize bible verses while I'm brushing my teeth. I'm going to brush my teeth anyway, and that's a good two minutes or so I can do something else. Here's another example—say you want to practice reading self-development material for at least 10 minutes a day. Well, download the audiobook and listen to it while you're doing the dishes or taking a drive.

Ask yourself, "What do I want to do while I'm doing [existing habit] to be more intentional?"

You can get creative with this and try all kinds of interesting things associated with a habit you already have. For example, some people like to walk on the treadmill while watching their favorite television show, associating new exercise with an already established viewing routine. Or you can practice learning a new language while putting away the laundry, something that you have to do anyway. As Kyle said, "It's a little thing, but it's a powerful concept. If you can take something that's already a habit and connect something new to it, it builds a habit. It's a very simple but practical shift that can make a big difference for people."

It doesn't always have to be at the same time, by the way. You can also make an effective link between an old habit and a new one by doing the new one immediately before or after. For example, after brushing your teeth every morning, maybe you practice meditation. Or maybe when you get up out of bed, you immediately put on your gym clothes to work out.

Any old habit can be the key to a new one.

Key Takeaways

Here are the key takeaways about getting into a routine that sets you up for success:

- Small daily actions add up and cumulatively make a huge difference in your life in the long run.
- Every little thing you do matters.
- The NFL training process is an extreme example of a straightforward, structured routine designed for success.

- We need to create a routine and structure that works for us individually.

- High performers from different walks of life have found similar success routines, including exercise, gratitude practice, silence, and intention.

- Your intention is essential to taking control of your day.

- Gratitude changes everything for the better.

- Being intentional the night before can help your next day go smoother.

- Find the things that move the needle in your life—they can be different for everyone.

- Practicing habit stacking can help you learn and keep new habits faster.

8 Starting Your Day with Wins and Building Momentum

The rhythm of daily action aligned with your goals creates the momentum that separates dreamers from super-achievers.

—Darren Hardy

Ever have one of those days where you feel completely unstoppable?

We've all had them at one point or another—a day you seem to rack up win after win after win, and nothing is slowing you down. It's a beautiful feeling, isn't it? Each success seems to fuel the next one, and before you know it, you have an unrestrainable momentum that takes on a life all its own.

In football, and sports in general, we strive for that kind of momentum, and we recognize that feeling on the field when it happens. It's not any single moment—it's when one team is successful in several events in a row, which leads the crowd and team to believe that more winning events are about to occur.

Just like in football, our life momentum comes from a series of events stacked on top of each other over time. When you start racking up wins through your consistent morning routine, you inevitably build positive momentum in your life. That routine you devised sets you up for success and is a promise you keep to yourself.

The momentum from all those actions will build in your life. Practiced long enough, you'll hit the "hockey stick effect"—a term often used in finance to record results over a long period. They call it a hockey stick because, on a graph, it looks flat for a long time, and then results rise dramatically in a very short time, creating the shape of a hockey stick. Remember in Chapter 7 I talked about how little micro-actions build up cumulatively over time? It's that effect measured, a phenomenon discussed in Jeff Olson's *The Slight Edge* and many other books on self-development. Your little wins will keep building over time until you break out with incredible results. Some success stories reflect the hockey stick effect in a short time, and others are years in the making.

However, there is a vital ingredient to maximize the potential of each win, no matter how big or small. First, you must record and recognize the win so that you can add it into your collective energy and the greater momentum of your life. And for you to do that, you'll have to start recognizing wins in your day-to-day life.

How Small Wins Add to Your Momentum

So, what is a "win"?

A win is an accomplishment with a beginning, a middle, and an end, and you feel good about it. It doesn't matter how big or small it is. It is an accomplishment that makes you feel better about yourself or makes you progress toward a stated goal, even if just a little bit. A little win can be an incremental step toward a larger win. Brushing your teeth can be a win. So can getting a huge promotion or being triumphant at the Super Bowl. It could be one piano practice or a successful recital. It can be one workout, or it could be losing 30 pounds over six months.

You are producing wins every day, and you might not even know it if you don't record or notice what's happening! For example, did you pay the bills? Did you go to work? Did you get some exercise? All wins!

You're losing out on enormous potential if you don't stop and measure your wins as progress in the overall goals of your life. Moreover, you're robbing yourself of momentum and joy that can get you there faster and be exciting and fun along the way.

If you take stock of your wins every day and see what you are accomplishing, your entire mindset will change. That's part of why I feel the morning routine is so crucial for your long-term and short-term success. And when you get to the end of the day, writing down all the wins and remembering all the things you are grateful for can give you a meaningful boost.

We all have rough days. It's easy to forget all the good you did throughout the day that aligns with your purpose, vision, and mission statement.

Start recording wins day by day as little positive markers, and your outlook on life will start to change.

It's funny; I didn't recognize the power of starting your day with wins until they were suddenly absent from my life. Only then did I have to get intentional about creating my own system and recording the wins as I went along.

Building Confidence Through Wins

The importance of recording your daily wins is something that high-performance people have recognized for years, especially in sports. I had the privilege of hosting Dr. Jason Selk on my podcast, a world-class coach and one of the top performance coaches in the United States. He's also a prolific author who shares many of his winning techniques in his books. Dr. Selk's specialty is mental toughness, which is of particular interest to people in athletics and the business world.

On my show, Dr. Selk had a fascinating perspective on why recording your wins are so essential for his brand of mental toughness. He said that whenever someone works with him, whether it's an athlete or an executive, this is where he starts—the foundation of his work:

The foundation of mental toughness is that you must learn to recognize when you're doing something well. . . . Unless an individual does learn to recognize what they've done well, discouragement is inevitable.

I agree. We need that self-encouragement to build our confidence. And if we're not actively recording those wins every day, then we're simply building discouragement and actively deflating momentum. If you're not encouraging yourself, you're discouraging yourself, and that's horrible for your confidence and long-term self-esteem:

The number one variable for all human performance is confidence. . . . You've got to retrain your brain. Instead of "you do a hundred things well and one thing less than perfect." A normal person at the end of the day, all they do is overlook all the things they did well and zero in on that imperfection . . . that is a pure sign of mental weakness.

If we're not in the habit of encouraging ourselves with wins, we are likely beating ourselves up unnecessarily. It's okay to recognize areas where we need to improve, but there's no honor or benefit from ignoring all the things we did well to fixate on that error or mistake. Dr. Selk insists that we start with what we did well and physically write three things down. By doing that, he says,

What it does is it starts to retrain your brain, so instead of looking at all the things you were imperfect with, you start by building a foundation where you say, "Hey, listen, I may not be perfect, but I'm doing this well, and this well . . . and that should count for something."

If you stick to this plan and take stock of everything you're doing well, your confidence will grow immeasurably. As Dr. Selk points out, "Focus on what you do well, and you'll do more of it well."

Some of the world's top performers take this advice. You can make it work wonders for you, too.

How Morning Wins Can Help You Mitigate Small Setbacks

By going through the powerful morning routine that you have created, you're stacking wins to start the day. You're putting yourself in a mindset to attack the day and be successful throughout the rest of your waking hours. You'll start out with more patience based on a little bit of quiet time. You're not rushing into things, not starting your morning in a reactive state.

You're essentially leaving nothing on the table. You're preparing for this day the best and most complete way you can. If something goes wrong, it's not because you didn't prepare properly or weren't in the right state of mind. One way I like to think about it is that if

I didn't do everything I could to prepare for a football game correctly, and we ended up losing the game, I would feel terrible. But if I knew in my heart that I prepared as hard as I could, then I could live with the loss. That's just football.

Similarly, when you prepare properly in ordinary life, and things still don't go your way, you can live at peace with it. You have done everything you could, and tomorrow is another day. I think that's a great analogy for life in general. If you're setting yourself up for success through your preparation and you're doing everything you can, that's all you can do.

It's essential to be kind to yourself and not beat yourself up too much when things go wrong, especially things that are out of your control.

I had Merril Hodge, a former professional football player and now an analyst for ESPN, on my podcast. He had a great story about not judging others or yourself too harshly. Merril said that he feels like he's a great little league football coach because he evaluates the kids based only on the "yardstick of their life." That was the term he used because if you try to treat a six- or seven-year-old on a football field the same way you do a college player, you're just expecting too much of them. However, if you're judging them based only on the point of life they are in presently, it becomes a lot easier.

Similarly, you can't judge yourself or expect too much of yourself when you did everything you could to prepare for the day properly. Sometimes, you'll have minor setbacks, and you can't take them personally. Just remember to apologize when necessary and check your pride at the door.

Remembering Big Wins Can Get You Through Significant Setbacks

Of course, some days, you have a more significant than usual setback, one that can send you reeling off course or spiraling into a dark place.

I'm not talking about losing your temper or being late to work. I mean terrible things, like losing your job, having a horrendous personal injury, or getting awful news from a friend or relative. Those are the days you have to pull out the big guns and remind yourself of times you conquered similar adversity.

Adversity can be such a tremendous gift. It makes us dig in and show ourselves what we are made of to conquer it. But, of course, the conquer part of it, the persevering through challenging circumstances, is the win. So when you see adversity again, it's no stranger to you. You'll know what you have to do because you've already done it in the past. That's why it's vital to remember the challenging things you've already been through—that you are strong, and this won't be the first big obstacle or the last that you must defeat.

Gaining Momentum from Wins Requires Accountability

Back in the days at the Bills' training facility, we would often go over the footage of our team's performance to determine how we could improve. The game tape was excellent—the camera doesn't lie. If my foot was in the wrong place, we didn't run the play according to the assignment, or we didn't communicate as a team, it was all up there on the tape. It always told the truth, and we could extract multiple wins from improving our performance from there. Having such a black-and-white metric was fantastic. Not repeating mistakes you have made is one of the greatest momentum builders and should be a constant focus in your life.

I don't have that game tape anymore to evaluate the metrics of my life, so I have to develop my own. Those little data points help me gain momentum from one week to the next.

One of the greatest allies I have in that arena is my personal executive coach, Mac. I tell Mac my goals, mission statement, what I want to be in life, and the things that I feel are obstacles in my way. When you are that honest, you almost force yourself into a certain standard. Mac helps me to hold myself accountable to my high standards. There's no avoiding it now; I put it out in the open! I know he's going to ask me whether I completed the task that I gave myself last week and all the other things that I know I need to be held accountable for.

That's why telling other people your goals can be a great thing—another tool to keep yourself accountable. For example, if a friend of mine knows I'm trying to lose weight, and he sees me eating a bunch of junk, he might stop me and ask, "Hey, Eric, what the heck are you doing? This isn't matching what you said you wanted." But, of course, if I had never said anything about my weight, then he probably wouldn't bring it up. And that's the point—people holding you accountable are your allies and will help you stack up the bigger wins you are shooting for.

One of my favorite quotes is from former college football player and current motivational speaker Inky Johnson, who tragically lost motor function in one of his arms after a hit that occurred in a football game, "Commitment is staying true to what you said you were going to do long after the mood that you said it in has left." It's human nature to stray off the course of our goals and vision, but having others who know what you're striving for can be a powerful force to keep you on your path to success.

Mac gave me a great tool to help me measure how I'm doing with my wife every week. He told me to ask her how I was doing as a husband every week on a scale of 1 to 10 (10 being the highest). Leslie would give me the number and sometimes an explanation of why she scored it that way. Then, my job was to make no excuses, try not to take it personally if it was low, and make my best efforts to work on raising it or keeping it high for the next week. That competitive nature makes me want to keep that score high, and all the competitive ones out there reading this love a scoreboard!

Plus, of course, I love Leslie, and I want to keep her happy and our relationship solid. So sometimes, if it's in the middle of the week, if I feel that maybe I'm not doing so well with her, I'll send her a text and say, "Hey, how are things going?" That check-in can go a long way and enables me to improve if needed.

Bottom line, if you want to improve your short-term and long-term life to help accumulate even more wins, you have to be honest about your present performance. You'll have to develop a system to get some kind of regular accountability.

Boundaries and Systems: Built-In Accountability for Wins

Some things are so ingrained in me that they become hard and fast rules or permanent systems. They are rules I will never break. Some of them relate to my core values and mission statement or my non-negotiables. Others relate to my short- and long-term goals, like maintaining a healthy weight. Some of them are just healthy habits I've formed as part of my morning routine.

Every time you choose to follow your built-in system or boundary is a win! You are aligning yourself in real time with the path for success that you have worked so hard on. It's staying on that freeway to your goals, rather than going off-roading and getting stuck and not knowing how to get out.

Any psychologist will tell you that it's an integral part of mental health to have definitive boundaries and to know there are certain lines you will just not cross. A friend I admire named Junior Bridgeman recently had a great expression about this.

Junior Bridgeman is an incredible guy. We play golf often, and I've hosted him on my podcast. Junior is an enormously successful businessman and former NBA player. He's the second-richest NBA player in the world behind Michael Jordan, except he earned most of that money from a restaurant empire, not his NBA career earnings. He has one of the best reputations, if not the best reputation, of anyone I've met in my entire life.

I asked Junior, "How have you been able to keep such an impeccable reputation your whole life where no one says anything bad about you?" I thought that inevitably, someone has got to have a bad experience with him, even if it may not have been his fault.

"I just have guardrails in my life," Junior replied, "and I never go outside those."

That answer blew me away because I couldn't believe the simplicity of it. I thought it was great advice, and I joked that maybe my guardrails were a little wider than his.

Guard rails are essentially the same as systems and boundaries to keep you on track. They can do wonders in cutting down on decision fatigue. If your system is strong enough, there won't be a decision to make at all! It would just be automatic behavior based on the rules you set for yourself.

That automatic, correct behavior helps me cut down on decision fatigue. For example, if I'm on an established system where I control my eating in a certain way, I don't have to worry about what I will eat tomorrow. I have already purchased the healthy food I want to eat, and the unhealthy food won't even be in my house. I don't have to worry about when I'm going to get up because I have my routine and alarm all set. And because I like to set up my next day the night before, I even have my clothes picked out.

The more I can have automatic guard rails in my life, the better. My mind races constantly, so anything that can stop me from a rabbit hole of indecision is excellent. I can put my systems on autopilot and let them take care of the small things.

At this point, my morning routine is part of that autopilot, and that's a great thing because that's the first of three essential ingredients to maintaining unstoppable momentum.

Maintaining Unstoppable Momentum Part 1: Daily Process

Once your daily process is set, and you've acquired the habit of doing it every day, you have created the foundation for building momentum. You're doing all the micro-actions necessary throughout the day and stacking wins on top of each other. You are also imperceptibly improving every day. You may not notice it at the moment, but over time it becomes undeniable.

Remember the hockey stick effect mentioned in Chapter 7? Where the measurement of your results looks flat for an extended period of time and then rises dramatically in a very short time? A parallel analogy for that dramatic rise is compound interest. In this comparison, we'll talk about percentage increases in improvement rather than money. So, if you get 1% better every day, you might think you are 365% better than at the start of the year, or roughly just over 3½ times more improved. That's great!

But that's not the actual number. The way compounding interest works is that you're 1% better than the day before, so you're actually 1% better than that new improved you that was 1% better than the day before that—and so on. So you're constantly improving by 1% something that was already improved. By the end of the year, you're actually 37 times more improved than your original baseline at the start!

That's the power of incremental improvement and stacking small wins every day. You will feel the little victories in the short term and big wins in the long term.

Relentless forward momentum doesn't have to be dramatic— every day doesn't have to light the world on fire! It can be just getting those little wins in the morning every day. So you keep moving forward, little by little.

My head coach when I got to the University of Louisville was Bobby Petrino. He said that in life, and in football, whatever you're doing, you're either getting better or getting worse. There's no gray area. So for people who are serious about getting further in life, there's no "I don't need to move forward today." You're not going to say, "I'll just stay where I am." That's not how things work. You're either moving in one direction or the other.

Every day doesn't have to be an absolute home run or swing for the fences because you'll probably crash and burn with that mentality. It's the little wins in the morning and throughout the day and then keeping track of those at night that allows you the peace of knowing that you're at least growing.

To bring it back to how momentum works in football, all the players are coming into the game field-ready from their daily routine over the last year. At the very minimum, they come in prepared and ready to go. Their daily process was never a question; it's what got them there and long predated running out of the tunnel at the start of the game. When you're watching a football game, the game doesn't actually start that day. The players began the game months and years ago at the beginning of their physical training journeys.

When they do come running out of that tunnel, they have already started to feel the second vital part of maintaining momentum—the roaring support of their fans.

Maintaining Unstoppable Momentum Part 2: Support System

One of the greatest joys and rushes from playing football is the support from the fans. There are so many times in a football game when our home fans gave us incredible support in critical moments. It is noticeably easier for the home team to feel and maintain their momentum because a gigantic crowd shouts their lungs out behind them. When you score a touchdown, and the crowd starts roaring, that momentum is tangible. It's one of the most incredible feelings in sports.

Conversely, the opposing team, when they feel that energy against them, might think, "We're in trouble now." They're going to be listening to the crowd and think it's going to be harder to build a successful offensive series because of the energy and that they won't even be able to hear each other out on the field. There's a pronounced momentum shift.

Similar to being out on the field in a game, you have a home team advantage when you have a support system in your corner and rooting you on. If you have a healthy support system in life, the right people supporting you along your journey, they will assist you immeasurably. If you have friends and family that genuinely want you to have success in life, they can help you build that momentum.

Professional athletes recently got a keen sense of the impact crowd energy has while playing during the pandemic. There were no crowds in NFL stadiums during the pandemic. I've heard firsthand from players how difficult it was to build and feel the momentum, even when doing well.

Remember how I mentioned that your friends sometimes have a better idea of your gifts than you do? The same goes for your wins. To you, it may have just been another day at the office. Your friends might see something entirely different: a responsible, capable superstar who handles themselves with confidence and grace. Often your support system might recognize small wins that you might not be fully celebrating or notice at all.

You can cultivate your home team advantage by selecting and leaning into your support system. I would encourage people to surround themselves with people who spur them on in their big and little moments. If you have that crowd celebrating with you, you're going to feel more momentum in your life. That could be from an executive coach, a life coach you hire, a spouse, your children, your buddies, mentors, teachers—it can come from all kinds of different places.

Your support system is your home team advantage when it comes to momentum. So make sure you explore it, use it, and appreciate it!

Maintaining Unstoppable Momentum
Part 3: Removing Distractions

Sometimes you have to add things to your life to help maintain or build your momentum. And sometimes, you have to subtract. One of the most important things that you can remove are distractions—useless wastes of time that get in the way of your goal. And in today's society, distractions are everywhere, coming at us from all directions.

If you don't limit distractions in your life, you may not even notice the momentum you already have, or worse, you can lose momentum, or you may not be able to create it. Those distractions can be internal or external, each of which produces a distinct challenge to overcome.

You can manage your distractions with a dedicated commitment to your morning routine. Those moments of silence and intentionally designing your day can go a long way in reminding you what you are doing, why you are here, and what you have set out to achieve today. In addition, I always find it grounding when I repeat the question I started the day with: "What good am I going to do today?"

Another great thing to manage internal distractions is to do your best to remain in the moment. No good can come from fixating on something that went wrong two minutes ago. If you were on a sailboat, I'd say that wind has already shifted. The wind from two minutes ago is gone. So adjust your sails accordingly.

External distractions in your own life present their unique maddening challenges. Getting a healthier relationship with your electronic devices is a great start.

Temptations in the form of food, a night out with friends, your favorite tv show, or even beautiful weather can throw you off track of what you are trying to do that day. So, return to your core values, mission, and how you decided your day was going to go today. Do you want to capitalize on your momentum, or do you want to derail yourself?

Certainly, we all know that certain distractions are unavoidable and an unfortunate fact of life. If someone you love is in bad shape, or you had a recent loss, or you are suffering some kind of injury or illness or abuse—those are life conditions that you have to deal with emotionally. There are beautiful distractions that are unavoidable, too—such as the birth of a new child or great news from your family. Make sure you give yourself space to deal with all of that—it's just part of life.

There's one more distraction that I would classify as internal and is insidious and tough to deal with. It's that inner voice that says you should quit when things get difficult. It's wanting to take the easy way out when you feel challenged outside your comfort zone. The internal voice sets up an internal battle inside yourself between two powerful forces—your standards versus your feelings.

Standards over Feelings

My friend Ben Newman, a renowned performance coach, global speaker, and bestselling author, said on my recent podcast that one of his secrets to success and forward momentum was executing "standards over feelings."

What he means is that if you let your feelings dictate how you operate, then you're always going to come up short because your feelings will derail you from the awkwardness of stretching outside your comfort zone to return to more safe or familiar circumstances. For example, if you are on a weight loss journey, you will feel hungry and feel like eating. If you are training to increase your stamina while running, that first mile outside your former limit will seem strange and difficult. Your feelings will want you to stop.

In the football season, there were days when I felt tired, achy, or worn out. I sometimes felt that it would be another monotonous day, and I just didn't want to push any further. But I didn't surrender to that feeling because I had a high standard.

Plus, your body likes to trick you into thinking it's exhausted when you still have much more strength and stamina left over in the tank. David Goggins, an ultramarathon runner and a former Navy SEAL, has some illuminating opinions of the body's limits. He said that in Navy SEAL training, when your body wants to quit, and when your mind and feelings tell you to quit, you're essentially only at about 40% of your capacity. You still have 60% left.

My buddy David Nurse says it takes about 17 seconds of discomfort to get used to something, and he uses a cold shower as an example. He also brings this up when he's training with NBA players. He'll say, "I know you're sore today, but just let's start this drill." And David says it usually takes about 17 seconds for them to get used to it. However, it could be anything, not just athletics. It could be the 17 seconds of discomfort you get from the heat of a sauna. Or it could be putting in a demanding workday. It could be sitting down to write a book! You just have to get through those first 17 seconds.

Whatever your unmotivated or uncomfortable moment might be, if you can get yourself past your feelings and push through, there is so much growth that can come from that, and that's amazing. You'll get more momentum if you work through these occasional bouts of discomfort. It's just part of the game.

Don't Let Positive Momentum Seduce You (Keep Doing the Thing!)

It was easy to get seduced by the positive momentum of the active season in football and let up a little on the off-season. But if you're a professional player, you have to keep your level of conditioning high and your strength high even during the months of the year that you're not playing. I always say that it's easier to stay ready than to get ready. During the season, the game may be getting easier for you because you are in the flow of things, but it's still vitally important you focus on getting better each day; you have to be careful not to plateau and think, "I've got this." Throughout the season, you should be improving and your techniques should be advancing.

Then the football season ends, which can be a giant momentum killer for your body. If you weren't plateauing before, here's when you might end up losing your momentum if you're not intentional about it. If you stick with your training and everything else during the off-season, hopefully, you can lock in where you are at. But I've seen so many guys go the opposite direction and completely kill their momentum. If you self-sabotage yourself, don't train in the off-season, or don't mentally prepare and actively seek ways to improve your craft, you're possibly going to be in worse shape than where you started the year before. Because, guess what? All the guys you are competing against are getting better, too!

The same lesson is applicable outside of athletics. If you build momentum, make this big sale, or complete this challenging project, you can be seduced by your own success and let your foot off the gas pedal a little bit. Maybe you take too much time off. Or you stop doing all your sales calls and aren't doing your homework correctly. Well, if you sit back and rest on your recent success, stop doing the daily things that got you there in the first place, and stop stacking those wins, you may find yourself going backward. You can lose all that momentum again. That's not the trajectory you want to be on.

Overcoming Negative Momentum

What happens when you start to feel momentum going in the wrong direction? Getting derailed might take you off your routine and your wins for a couple of days, which could turn into weeks and months. Or perhaps you became seduced by your success and got a little sloppy with your routine. Then, suddenly, you might find yourself going in the wrong direction fast.

The first thing I would recommend is not to beat yourself up and just get back on the routine as soon as possible. I've seen this a lot with people on their weight loss journeys. Maybe they had terrific momentum and just lost 15 pounds, then they break their routine over one weekend and gain back five practically overnight. Sometimes there's discouragement there or thought that all this effort wasn't worth it. Perhaps they feel like they're not getting quick-enough results, or maybe they're beating themselves up about feeling like a failure.

Again, be kind to yourself. Sometimes there are setbacks, but it doesn't mean you can't get back on the wagon. Forgive yourself, think about strategies to prevent the same kind of backsliding from happening again, and move on. Expect to have a little discomfort getting back to where you were and just keep going.

For example, no matter how much I trained, I sometimes felt like I had backslid during the off-season. The first place I would feel the sorest was my neck, which is typical for many players. Generally, when you start a training camp, your neck will be sore. It's from holding this heavy helmet on that your body has to be accustomed to again. You're taking shots to the head and your neck all the time as an offensive lineman, so you have to train to get used to it again. That's part of the reason why you see football players walking around with these big traps and thick necks.

You also have to train your neck in the off-season to be able to withstand that. You don't quit over a sore neck, just like you don't stop if you have a setback. Instead, just like regaining neck strength, you'll build up your skill level again and return to your peak capability.

Growing Your Confidence and Process Goals

The other thing I have to remind myself of is that following my daily routine, in and of itself, is a win. It's what's known as a process goal. Dr. Selk and I talked about that when I hosted him on my podcast. He said the second key ingredient to building your confidence is focusing on process goals.

So what is a process goal? Process goals are very well known in the sports world among coaches. To define them, it helps to compare process goals against product goals, otherwise known as results. As Dr. Selk pointed out, a product goal can be something like winning the Super Bowl or earning $100,000 this year. There's nothing wrong with having a product goal. They are highly motivating.

Process goals, however, are daily activities that help you fulfill your product goals. Dr. Selk defines a process goal as "What is the single most important activity that will cause the result you are looking for?" For instance, for his Super Bowl example, Dr. Selk suggests it might be at the very least making 100% of the practices. For the $100,000 example, it might be focusing on seven key sales calls every single day.

Once again, it all comes back to the daily routine. That's where your process lives. And as Dr. Selk points out: "If you focus on the process, you have control of the result."

Looking Back at How Far You've Come

Your routine, your process goals, and your wins will continue to sharpen your sword in all areas of life, build momentum, and ultimately help you become the person you want to be. As you grow, don't be surprised that certain things will start to change. When you gain one thing in life, you lose another. The reverse is also true—when you lose one thing in life, you also gain another.

Applied to your life, adding your new daily routine means you will likely lose activities you were doing at that time—subtracting things that weren't intentional. And as you become proficient in your new daily routine and gain momentum, you'll find new activities that will enhance your journey and lead toward exciting growth. All this intentionality will inevitably lead to a noticeable change in your life.

Change isn't always easy. As you become successful, some people might see a negative connotation concerning improvements in your life, such as a new relationship or accumulating wealth. It's completely normal to change—it's unhealthy not to! If you haven't seen someone in five years, and they're the same person they were then, it doesn't reflect well on them. I think it would benefit all people to be super-learners, avid acquirers of new knowledge until the Lord calls you home.

You should be changing continually, building on your momentum, and constantly enhancing yourself as a work in progress.

Key Takeaways

Here are the key takeaways about starting your day with wins and building momentum:

- Stacking and recording small wins add to your momentum.
- You can build your confidence with small wins.
- Small wins are little accomplishments with a beginning, middle, and end.
- Wins can help you mitigate small and significant setbacks.
- Gaining momentum from wins requires accountability.
- Boundaries and systems create built-in accountability for wins.
- The first key ingredient to maintaining your momentum is sticking to your daily routine.

- The second key ingredient to maintaining your momentum is a strong support system.

- The third key ingredient to maintaining your momentum is eliminating distractions.

- It's crucial to uphold standards over feelings when struggling with discomfort.

- Don't let positive momentum seduce you into falling out of your routine.

- Forgive yourself any setbacks from negative momentum, and get back into your routine.

- Keep growing your confidence with process goals—if you control the process, you control the result.

- Adding one thing into your life sometimes means subtracting another and vice versa.

- Take stock of how much you've grown and how far you've come in your journey.

9 Serve Others

A generous person will prosper; whoever refreshes others will be refreshed.

—Proverbs 11:25

What if the secret to a joyful, prosperous life is taking the focus off of yourself and putting it on how you can serve and help other people?

It's an intriguing idea, yet it may seem counterintuitive, especially when you may be in your lowest moments and feel you need the most help yourself. When you're in a transition period, and you're looking for your next chapter in life, you might say, "How does serving others help me here?" It's hard to see past your situation when you're in the middle of it.

What if using our unique gifts to go out and have an impact on others brings us the most clarity and satisfaction in life? And what if serving others inevitably makes us more wildly joyful and prosperous than we could imagine? And what if finding your unique way to serve others and bring value to them was the secret to bringing you financial success as well?

I believe serving others is the ultimate secret to success. I feel I am living proof of that. Yet, it took quite a journey for me to come to that conclusion.

How I Came to Adopt a Serving Others Mentality

In 2012 I was having lunch with a good friend of mine, Ronnie Cordrey. Ronnie is the head of Men's Ministry at Southeast Christian Church, one of the largest churches in the United States. Here's the thing about Ronnie—he lived with more joy than anybody I had ever seen. It just permeates out of his body. So when I peeled back the layers on that (and I know everybody, including Ronnie, has their struggles in life), I felt like he modeled joy better than anyone I had ever seen. I asked him what the secret to all of his joy was.

He said he tried to live by Proverbs 11:25, which states, "a generous person will prosper; whoever refreshes others will be refreshed." He said someone challenged him to live by this, and he challenged me to do the same. Ronnie explained just to try and be as generous as possible in life, and, ultimately, I would always be rewarded back.

After that fateful lunch, I went home and wrote it down. I studied it and committed it to memory. And each day since, that's been my philosophy in life. I look to build others up. I've committed myself to deepening my generosity, and I strive to be more generous with my time, talent, and treasure. As a result, we've seen so many blessings come back to us—sometimes in the form of tangible gifts or financial blessings and other times it's simply feeling joy and fulfillment that I've helped someone else with something I had to offer.

It's been 10 years since that meeting. I felt a big switch back then, and I'm still talking about that meeting because it was a pivotal moment for me, and made everything just click. Honestly, Ronnie's whole personality was full of so much joy it made it easy to stick with. I wanted to live like that, too! It was amazing to watch how resilient he was and his impact on so many men in our community and our church. It made me want to make an impact through the platforms I had available and the gifts God gave me.

I started to become a better leader within our team. I began to feel like I was more of an asset to my family. I suddenly felt like I was a better friend, and it changed my whole mindset on generosity.

It's good that the idea was so branded into my brain because I would be tested when I lost my football career. It took some powerful reminders that, even during adversity, generosity and serving others was the right path.

My Challenges with Serving Others After My Pivot Point

I was so grateful for the job I had with the Bills, my family, my salary, my friends, and so much more. Then, after my injury, my career was gone.

So there was a new uncomfortable question I had to ask myself: "You were making more money than you thought possible, and it seemed easier to be generous then. Now, can you live by it? When football is taken away?"

It was a confusing time, and I truly felt I was probably not focused on serving others as much as I should have been because I was so concerned with what would come next for me. About this time, when I first started the podcast, one of my first guests was Chris Burke, a former Major League baseball player from Louisville, Kentucky. Chris had already blazed a trail transitioning from professional baseball to his retired life and shared incredible insight.

At some point during the podcast interview, Chris said something I would never forget: "Focus on serving others, and it will make this transition to your next chapter so much easier." When I heard him speak those words so clearly, it was as if Proverbs 11:25 lived inside of me again, and it hit home. My mind shifted from "What am I going to do next to prove to other people that I'm worthwhile on this earth now that my football career is gone?" to "How can I use my gifts to serve others?"

Thinking about all the lives I could affect positively and all the people I could serve helped everything I was doing be *about* something much more important than just my career.

The Long-Term Benefits of Generosity and Serving Others

It's a nice thing to think that generosity often comes back to you. The ironic thing is that a generous heart isn't doing it for the benefit. The giving itself should be its own reward. Nonetheless, pure altruism and serving others almost always yield other rewards, too. Long-term studies have shown time and again the tremendous benefits of being generous with your friends, family, colleagues, and the larger community.

Some studies suggest that generosity and service in the form of volunteerism may extend one's life. For example, the John Templeton Center at UC Berkeley produced a research paper in May 2018 entitled "The Science of Generosity." In it, they note the surprisingly positive impact of generosity on mortality:

A study that analyzed data from a nationally representative sample of 1,211 Americans over the age of 65 found that volunteering was associated with delayed death. (p. 20)

The same research paper found that giving social support is more beneficial to your mortality than receiving it:

When it comes to generosity and health, it really may be better to give than to receive. A study of patients with end-stage renal disease found that those who gave more social support—be it through social interaction, material aid, advising, or emotional support—to friends and family were significantly less likely to die over a 12-month period, whereas those who received social support were no more or less likely to die. (p. 20)

Serving others doesn't have to look like volunteerism or even grand gestures of social support. Sometimes it is smaller, simple acts such as giving emotional support to your spouse or helping out with the housework. Altruistic acts like these are also a service and great for extending your life. The study explains:

Another study looked at the effects of giving and receiving emotional support (such as making their spouse feel loved and cared for or listening to them when they needed to talk) and instrumental support (such as help with transportation, child care, housework, etc.) on mortality among older married couples from the Detroit area. After controlling for a number of variables, including the health of the participants, the researchers found that people who reported providing more emotional support to their spouse and/or instrumental support to friends, relatives, and neighbors had a significantly reduced death rate during the five-year period, compared with those people who had reported offering less support. (p. 20)

In our work lives, multiple studies confirm that generosity is essential to retaining happiness at work. For example, the University of Wisconsin–Madison's La Follette School of Public Affairs had their research summarized in their 2013 in-house article "Virtue Rewarded: Helping Other People at Work Makes People Happier" in 2013:

the authors find that individuals in their mid-30s who rated
helping others in their work as important said they were
happier with their life when surveyed again almost 30 years
later. . . . "It's exciting that in both tests, our measures of
altruism had relatively large effects on happiness," Moynihan
says. "Being motivated to help and believing your work makes
a difference is associated with greater happiness in our
analysis."

Being generous and serving others is also good for our mental
health and immune systems and helps us build a social network and a
meaningful place in our community. In a 2010 *Psychology Today*
article titled "Generosity: What's in It for You?" author Lisa Firestone
first describes how acts of altruism are good for our overall health:

A 2003 research study at the University of Michigan reveals
that the positive effects of generosity include improving one's
mental and physical health and promoting longevity. In
another Michigan study, which traced 2,700 people over
10 years, researchers found that men who did regular
volunteer work had death rates two-and-one-half times lower
than men who didn't. Generosity reduces stress, supports one's
immune system and enhances one's sense of purpose.

She also explains that generosity causes others to return the favor,
with generous gestures acting as a multiplier that connects the
community at large:

Being built up with compliments has little effect on our self-worth, whereas the gratification of being generous enhances our sense of self. Furthermore, when we are in a giving state, we are more relaxed, attuned, and living in the moment. This state of being is contagious; people who are generous often create a snowball effect in others who in turn want to pay it forward.

Study after study confirm the measurably positive impacts of serving others and how it's great for your health, your work life, and the health and strength of the community at large. Let's run through those benefits again:

- Generosity toward others increases measurable feelings of happiness.
- Generosity in the form of volunteerism can extend your life.
- Giving social support is more beneficial to your mortality than receiving it.
- Small acts of emotional support and altruism also extend your life.
- Generosity is essential to retaining happiness at work.
- Being generous and serving others is good for your mental health, your immune system, and helps you build a meaningful place in your community.
- Being generous is contagious and has a positive snowball effect on others who want to pay it forward.

There is no downside to helping others, and science seems to confirm that. It's not just wishful thinking or new age sentiment.

Start focusing on others if you want to enjoy the finer things in life and a more fulfilling existence. It can only come back to you in return.

The Unexpected Benefits of Serving Even When You Are at a Pivot Point

Culturally, it is challenging because we live in a Western society, and there tends to be a selfish tendency in our attitude toward success. As a result, many of us want to see tangible returns. Yet, unlike traditional investments, which pay you tangible returns over a finite amount of time, your investment in service to other people often gets repaid in intangibles over your entire lifetime. Some of these intangibles you will never see on a balance sheet, but their positive impact on you are real and measurable.

Your relationships become incredibly enriched. If you pour your energy into others, especially your spouse or significant other, the benefits become immediate and exponential. And the two of you as a couple can only grow stronger. There's an amazing book that expands on the service mentality in successful relationships called *What Radical Husbands Do* by Regi Campbell. It's all about serving your spouse and how, with service, your relationship will prosper physically and emotionally like you never thought possible.

I've also found through serving others, I have become calmer, at peace, and satisfied with the good I was helping to become a reality. It also just feels right. I've been incredibly blessed, and I think it is only appropriate to help other people when I can.

If you are picking up this book in the middle of a transition period, and you're looking to make the next chapter in your life your best chapter, trust me on this point. Take the focus off yourself and pour your gifts and efforts into serving the world. Find ways to serve people within your chosen profession. At the very least, pour service and love into your friends, significant other, or spouse. The benefits will come back to you tenfold.

Once you see everything through the lens of service, the quality of your relationships will vastly improve. You will see all kinds of little opportunities to serve every day. I'll give a simple example in my own life. Every morning I prepare all the fixings for coffee on the counter so my wife Leslie can enjoy a hot cup of coffee. I don't do it out of expectation. I'm doing it because it's a little thing I can do every day to serve her. Inevitably, she'll do something sweet back in return to me, which just makes our relationship tighter.

All of these tiny acts of service inside a relationship add up into something much greater than the whole. When you start living like that every day, you're not going to have to pound Proverbs 11:25 into your head to remind you to be of service. It's just going to be there, like anything else you practice. It will become an innate routine and part of the way you see and interpret the world.

Anything you do repetitively that shows positive fruit in your life, you're going to want to keep doing. It becomes part of your DNA.

Finding Ways to Serve in All the Buckets of Your Life

Sometimes it's important to step back and see how you are already serving in the world. Ask yourself the question, "What good are you doing? How does your profession help people?" If you're having trouble figuring it out, remember that you wouldn't be getting paid for any job if it wasn't valuable or of service to somebody.

We have all lived through unprecedented times, when we are finally starting to recognize the importance of people who sell us groceries as essential workers, literally vital to keeping civilization fed and operative. Our context also changed to include many other professions as essential, such as delivery and mail people, garbage collectors, and janitors as essential workers alongside doctors and scientists. We literally cannot run society without them.

Similarly, anything you do, any task that you are paid for or is helpful to anyone, is a way to serve. If you get behind the mindset and intentional about that service, you'll find both your satisfaction and impact increase.

In order to light someone up and make a positive impact on them, you'll have to use your gifts. That's why one of the first chapters in this book is about recognizing your gifts. You'll need to have a clear idea of how you can contribute to be of service and maximize your impact on others. You'll have a certain clarity about where you belong and how you can be useful. Whatever your skill, you have an opportunity to serve.

There's a men's group that I serve each week at our church. I get to practice some of the leadership skills I learned in football, as well as my connecting ability, because I've always been social. I love working with them, seeing their relationships affected and their lives enriched with more joy. I get such tremendous gratification from that, knowing that I can help others around me who are trying to improve their lives. I just wanted to serve—the rewarding feelings just happened as a result.

I've had a similar experience with my podcast. At first, my guests were mainly other athletes with similar experiences to mine. As the show went forward, the focus shifted to learning from high performers in various industries. I wanted to create content that would uplift and have an impact on others. I've heard countless stories of people who have adapted something that they heard on the podcast.

In turn, every guest served me in some fashion. Even if it was a reciprocal deal where I would do something on one of their shows afterward, they still served my listeners and me with their time and knowledge.

Even with my sports broadcasting work, I like to feel motivated by how it serves other people. I know that people work hard all week, and they get to watch this football game. They love this game, just like I do, and I like to deepen their enjoyment by offering my analysis and giving them practical knowledge to get smarter about the game. I'm trying to project positive energy to enrich their experience.

I'm not one to hide my faith, so I like to point people to Christ when appropriate and when I can. As a result, I've brought many people to my church and have benefited from watching people deepen their relationship with God and their greater community. That is incredibly rewarding because I know I helped them start on a journey they'll be on for the rest of their lives.

Internal Challenges of a Serving Mentality

Being in service takes humility. That alone can be the biggest challenge for some people, especially those who have been successful for a long time and have been in the spotlight.

That humble posture is deceptive. To some people, it might appear they are lowering themselves, that it takes something away from their platform of influence. They're worried that humility and service might diminish them somehow. We can all take a page out of Jesus's playbook, credited as being the most influential person in history by many nonreligious publications, when he said that he "came to serve and not be served."

Sometimes people have a scarcity mentality, meaning they are afraid of losing status or wealth because there may not be enough to go around. They may also feel that uplifting others will come at a high personal cost, either in time or treasure, that they are not willing to part with.

Another objection is that people feel serving others might be inconvenient. And you know what? Sometimes it is inconvenient. Sometimes service puts you out of your comfort zone and puts you in situations in which you are entirely unfamiliar. However, I don't think that's a bad thing. On the contrary, I believe that the only times you truly grow are when you push yourself out of your comfort zone. Through that discomfort, you can find all sorts of discoveries and new ideas about how you can contribute and where you belong.

You'll always be glad that you did push yourself out of your comfort zone. It's in that area that you'll find a lot of those butterfly moments, those moments that are so enriching and where it's exciting to be alive. Butterfly moments may make you feel uneasy before they occur because you know you're stretching yourself, but you push through that uneasiness because you're going to love the feeling on the other side of it.

Servant Leadership

I've met many amazing people who model a servant's heart, and those who make service a priority in their lives make the best leaders. Servant leadership is a relatively new concept in the business world, the term gaining popularity in the last few decades. The idea is simple: a servant leader serves their followers and leads by example. A popular Christian example is that a shepherd serves his flock, much like a pastor serves his congregation.

In the business world, a servant leader serves the employees and is concerned with their personal welfare and growth as a priority. Servant leaders lead by example and strive to build strong relationships with everyone they work with. Such organizations usually have excellent retention because employees feel taken care of and thus have greater commitment. When servant leaders go out of their way to help their employees succeed, the employees are usually willing to return the favor for the organization.

I have found so many servant leaders in the sports world. Sean McDermott, the head coach of the Buffalo Bills, is a prime example. He would never expect his players or assistant coach to do anything he wasn't willing to do himself, including getting up early in the morning and going to work out, which seems like a tiny thing. But as a player, I can't tell you how impressive it is to see your head coach model the behavior he's asking from you by showing up before five in the morning to get a workout in first thing.

In the NFL, you end up having lots of paid assistants to help support you in getting into top form. You have physical and massage therapists, doctors, nutrition coaches, and a small army of people that help you take care of your equipment and even clean up after you. If you always have an assistant who does everything for you, it's easy to get lazy and forget about a service mentality.

When I first started at the Bills, we would take our tape off after practice and just sort of throw it on the floor or leave it lying around. I'm ashamed to say that I knew there were people whose job was to clean up the locker room, so I didn't think about it. And we would leave our tape, food, all kinds of trash in there for them to deal with.

Sean McDermott came into the building, shook his head, and said, "No, no, no. You guys put your own trash in the garbage. We clean up after ourselves. That's what we do." And then he told the equipment guys not to throw away our trash anymore. If their job was to handle the equipment, then Sean wanted them just to handle the equipment and not enable us to be lazy about trash. In retrospect, it's kind of a no-brainer and a little embarrassing to have to be told that. Yet, it goes to show you that we can get into lazy habits that get in the way of having a servant's heart.

When I entered the NFL, there was a practice that had been around for decades of hazing the incoming rookies. This could range from having them carry in your pads after practice to spending tens of thousands of dollars on a meal for their position group. In my rookie year, most, but not all, of the veterans made sure they had their fun with their first-round offensive lineman. Many of the ones who treated me like a teammate and not a subordinate I'm still friends with to this day.

I once heard of an NFC team that will remain nameless that the veterans would march the rookies around the dorms in the middle of the night so they were sure to wake up exhausted for two-a-day practices the next day. They would also throw guys in ice tubs with their wrists and ankles taped so they couldn't quickly get out. This team also competed for Super Bowls, so maybe there was a good method to their madness, but I wasn't comfortable doing those things.

Midway through my career, I sought to change the way we treated rookies. I was finding that as a leader of the team, the rookies were not responding well to me during games because they either didn't like me, didn't trust me, or had no relationship with me because of the hazing. We continued to do a big meal together once a year that the rookies would buy, but I would always tell the veterans not to order anything off the menu that they wouldn't get if they were buying, and I knew which cheapskates to call out quickly!

People don't care how much you know until they know how much you care. Instead of separating myself from the rookies, I would build relationships with them, and their performance and our performance as a team saw the benefit of that. I have friendships to this day that are a direct result of treating rookies better than they were traditionally treated in the NFL.

In my religious life, I've experienced servant leadership from David Stone and his wife, who have hosted us at a couples Bible study nearly every other week for at least six years now. They're constantly opening up their house to us and serving young couples. They'll talk about how they're refreshed by helping young couples. They know they have to walk the walk, and they enjoy doing it. They've been a game-changer in my life, helping me grow to become a better husband and father for my family. So I had them both on my podcast. I thought they had a lot to offer people about taking ownership of their lives and their marriage—they've been happily married for over 35 years.

Then there was Chris Burke, who originally served me in Men's Ministry at Southeast. I got to see this former professional athlete, a fantastic baseball player, being a dad and a husband living in Louisville, Kentucky. I constantly got to see that he modeled what it looked like to serve his family and his community through his church.

At the bottom of my stationery is a quote from Jackie Robinson, which reads, "A life is not important except for in the impact it has on others." I have always loved that quote. Servant leaders intuitively understand the importance of having an impact and seek to uplift others more than they do to aggrandize themselves.

Key Takeaways

Here are the key takeaways about serving others and approaching your life with a servant's heart:

- One of the secrets to a joyful, prosperous life is taking the focus off yourself and serving others.

- Proverbs 11:25 says, "A generous person will prosper; whoever refreshes others will be refreshed." The idea is any good you do will come back to you in some way.

- Service to others makes weathering personally difficult times more manageable and more meaningful.

- Numerous studies have indicated that generosity and service are good for your physical and emotional health, relationships, work life, community, social standing, and long-term mortality.

- You can make service part of your DNA by practicing it often. Then, over time, its positive fruits will reinforce your behavior to keep the practice.

- Look for ways to serve in all the buckets of your life.

- There are challenges to a service state of mind; it requires humility and the willingness to extend beyond your comfort zone. You also must overcome a scarcity mentality that there is not enough time or treasure to go around.

- Servant leaders make the best leaders. Common traits of service leaders are leading by example, putting their follower's needs and welfares above their own, and building strong relationships and partnerships based on the greater good of their community or organization.

10 Fill Your Mind with What You Want to Show Up in Your Life

Watch your thoughts, they become your words; watch your words, they become your actions; watch your actions, they become your habits; watch your habits, they become your character; watch your character, it becomes your destiny.

—Lao Tzu

As an athlete, I'm acutely aware of all the food and beverages I put into my body. It took me much longer to be conscious of a question I should have been asking all along: "What are you putting into your mind?"

That question may be the most significant thing you ever ask yourself. People who deliberately choose what they think about and fill their minds with positive thoughts that spark growth will be successful in all the buckets of life. Conversely, someone who lives their life on autopilot and fills their mind with whatever captures their attention is bound to have mediocre results.

Just as you are what you eat, you also become what you think.

How? It all sources from the mind. Your thoughts become your behavior, your behavior becomes your actions, and your actions become your future. It's as simple as that.

Of course, there's always a catch. To harness the power of your mind, you have to become disciplined and know how to steer it. And the entire world is full of obstacles that can easily knock you off course.

The Sea of Thoughts

One of the biggest obstacles is your own's mind incredible processing power and capacity for information. You are capable of thousands of thoughts every day. In the 2020 *Newsweek* article, "Humans Have More Than 6,000 Thoughts per Day, Psychologists Discover," Jason Murdock explains: "The researchers said the study shows how measuring thoughts can predict a person's personality, estimating the average human will have about 6,200 thoughts per day."

That is an incredible amount of noise created by our own minds and could be dangerous to our long-term future. If left undirected and open to any influence that comes along, distraction becomes inevitable.

What would it look like if most of those thoughts were constructive, conscious, and sending you in a positive direction? To do that, we have to consciously place a focused thought that we control and purposely curtail thoughts that send us astray. It is the idea of letting your intentions guide you throughout your day.

Self-Limiting Beliefs

One of the challenges all of us face, myself included, are negative thoughts sourced from inside our minds. Negative thoughts can come in infinite varieties, and I'm sure you'll recognize some of the most common ones:

- I'm not good enough.

- I'm a failure.

- I will never get this right.

- That person is better than me.

- I'll never be any good.

- I'm dumb.

- I'm weak.

- I'm inept.

- I can't do anything right.

There's another word for all this negative self-talk—self-limiting beliefs. Because that is all they are: a belief, not a fact, even though they may seem like facts. They are just beliefs that only seem real and don't serve you—you can just as easily replace them with more productive beliefs. And just like your self-limiting beliefs, positive beliefs about yourself increase potency with repetition. If you tell yourself "I'm a success" often enough, you will find a way to construct that future instead.

That's why you have to be extremely careful about what you tell yourself every day. And if you're not telling yourself anything, you're in trouble because you will let what is all around determine your direction instead of you. You're relinquishing your ship to the wind.

Psychologists are fully aware of the power of negative self-talk and how limiting and destructive it can be. In the *Psychology Today* article, "Self-Talk," written by the Psychology Today staff, they explain:

The problem with negative self-talk is that it typically does not reflect reality, and so it can convince people, wrongly, that they are not only not good enough, but that they can never get better, paralyzing them into self-absorption and inaction.

Filling your mind with negative self-talk will cause negative things to show up in your life. The good news is the reverse is also true. Practicing positive self-talk can help you turn things around. We'll get to techniques on how to do that in a moment. For now, take notice of any powerful self-limiting beliefs you may have. Are you letting them get in the way of what you want? Are you letting them stop you from your full potential?

You always have the power to replace negative self-talk with an affirmation—a positive statement about yourself that you declare. What if you replaced your negative self-talk and told yourself these messages instead?

- I'm good enough.
- I'm a success.
- I will get this right.
- I don't compare myself to other people.
- I will be good.
- I'm smart.
- I'm strong.
- I'm capable.
- I can take on challenges and succeed.

How different would your life look if this was the conversation you had with yourself every day?

The Power of Media

When it comes to filling your mind with what you want to show up in your life, your self-limiting beliefs are the first hurdle you must conquer, but not the only one. The second most significant thing that can distract you is all the external messages you receive from all forms of media.

I'm not saying all media is negative. I am saying that media is pervasive and everywhere, and if you're not careful, you might find yourself getting influenced in a way that is not helpful for your direction. These days media comes at us from all sides from all platforms, in entertainment, news, social media, and most of all advertising. Worse, it comes from devices we carry around with us everywhere. Even if you don't use a personal digital device, media is still omnipresent, in virtually every interior, and even coming at you from all directions when you're walking around outside. You also interact with brands and their associated brand identities every day through the things you already own: your clothes, your computers, your breakfast cereal, your home décor. All of it comes with an accompanying message.

Some experts believe that all that media bombardment can lead to widespread unhappiness, just from advertising alone. That conclusion doesn't surprise me in the least.

But why does advertising make us unhappy? Oswald, the scientist from the study, suspects it has to do with the dissatisfaction that comes with comparing your lifestyle to one that you feel is better than yours:

The idea here is a very old one: Before I can decide how happy I am, I have to look over my shoulder, consciously or subconsciously, and see how other people are doing. Many of

my feelings about my income, my car, and my house are
molded by my next-door neighbor's income, car, and house.
That's just part of being human: worrying about relative
status. But we know from lots of research that making social
comparisons can be harmful to us emotionally, and
advertising prompts us to measure ourselves against others.

When we add up all these influences of just the passive forms
of media consumption, like casually scrolling through social media
and advertising in all of its forms, it paints a scary picture. There is a
fight for your attention and mind, and if you don't choose what you
want to think about, the media environment will choose for you.

The Power of Choosing Your Thoughts

Internationally renowned motivational speaker Les Brown has a
powerful thing to say on the subject of your mind's attention. He
said, "Life is a fight for territory. And once you stop fighting for what
you want, what you don't want will automatically take over."

You have to claim the territory of your mind, or it will get filled
with whatever is the most pervasive. It can happen unwittingly before
you even know it.

In addition to all the passive forms of media consumption, there
are the media platforms you deliberately choose to consume. Your
music, movies, news, books, magazines, television shows, podcasts,
favorite websites, and whom you follow and network with on social
media are all your chosen forms of media consumption. You are solely
responsible for those choices.

News, for example, has the potential to be particularly damaging
to your mental health, depending on how you consume it. In the
2019 *Psychology Today* article "How Negative News Distorts Our

Thinking," Austin Perlmutter, MD, outlines the general doom and gloom effect it has on our mood:

Watch, read, or listen to the news, and you're likely to come away believing that the world is rapidly descending into disaster and chaos, even though many aspects of life have improved dramatically over the last few decades. Exposure to consistent, sensationalized pessimism and negativity has become the norm for those keeping up with the news.

This matters, because research shows us that what we see on the news can significantly impact our mental health. While negative news may influence our thinking through multiple mechanisms, one important consideration is how it interfaces with our cognitive biases, keeping our focus on everything that's going wrong while blinding us to all the good things around us.

It's not just hard news—even sports news or social media channels often have a negative bent. If you leave it up to chance, you're going to be consuming a lot of negative headlines, even if you're just reading sports. Most of the headlines want to maximize drama, and most drama is inherently negative in some fashion. They know what sells, what will get clicks, and these negative stories get incredible attention.

Be honest with yourself. Does any of the content you consume help you on your journey? Does what you consume align with the vision you have set up for yourself? Before you go any further, consider the answer to these questions:

- What's the first thing you listen to or watch or read when you first get up?

- What are your favorite tv shows, podcasts, movies, reading materials? Are they adding value to your life?
- How much time do you spend on media that doesn't uplift you?
- Where are your limits coming from?
- Is there information out there that you want to learn? What's stopping you from learning it?
- Is the content you're consuming worth the impact it has on your life? Even if it's just the time spent on it?
- How valuable is your time?

The whole point of these questions is to help you be aware and intentional of what you are putting into your mind. You could start your day with news of how awful the world is and how angry everyone is with each other, or you could create the story for the rest of the day another way. There is untold power in your morning routine, and that's why I keep hammering its importance—you could start the day and keep it going with whatever fuels your fire and moves you that much further along with your desired vision.

The alternative is throwing your fate to the wind. You can be cruising through your day on autopilot, and suddenly you may feel heavy and weighed down by all these negative thoughts. Autopilot is not a good place to be in because then you're not making any choices at all.

I can't emphasize enough to avoid autopilot at all costs. Too many people live on autopilot, and they just do the same thing, week after week. They don't quite understand the concept that it's thought patterns that become behaviors, which become actions, which become your future. Ultimately, you're going to be the sum of your actions.

So would you rather the world plant those words and ideas in your mind, or would you rather do it by choice?

How I Filled My Mind in College Football

Back when I was in college football, I was highly unintentional about what I was consuming. I wasn't necessarily a reader outside all the school work that I was consuming.

I was lucky to have constructive and positive messaging from my coaches, preventing me from going on autopilot completely. Fortunately for me, I played under coaches who could both push me and speak confidence into me. Of course, the pushing part isn't always fun, but I can honestly say that it created a toughness and level of intensity that raised my game and, ultimately, my confidence.

You are at the mercy of your coaches in college football and what they fill your mind with. When I came to college, I played for Bobby Petrino, who was on the rise, and rightfully so.

Part of what made Bobby Petrino a great leader was that he was very demanding and had high expectations of us. Sometimes that approach is required for players to rise to the occasion, but it wasn't easy. He wasn't that interested in building a relationship with us—his assistant coaches were more relational, which made it all work. Bobby demanded hard work and excellence in all that we did, and he backed it up himself by working tirelessly to prepare game plans that would set us up for success on the field.

He would put a lot of pressure on us to perform and would not shy away from letting us have it with his words, but it was because he wanted to push us toward greatness. He once asked us in a team meeting who wanted to play in the NFL after college. I believe every hand in the room went up. He then said, "Good, because you will not be able to withstand the coaching and work that you will be subjected to if you don't have high aspirations for yourselves." When you did receive a compliment from Bobby, it meant the world to you because he didn't hand them out carelessly or often.

That's the way Bobby would work—he was on a mission to win.

I was fortunate at that formative time in my life. I wasn't as intentional as I am now about my thoughts; however, I had incredible coaches, teachers, and mentors who filled that vessel with thoughts that would help me grow and stay on the right track. Some people don't emerge from their programs so lucky. That's one of the reasons it's essential to have strong leadership guiding our young minds.

How I Filled My Mind in the NFL

When I was in the NFL, I was just beginning to get into intentional practices for my thoughts. I didn't start right away. It took me a while to realize that I was in charge of my thoughts, and I couldn't leave it up to external forces.

I started to get better and better at intentionally filling my mind, and I'm so glad I did because it led me to get life coaching and a higher quality of feedback that I could use. I credit life coaching for helping me transition after my career-ending injury and guiding me to think about myself in different terms than just being a football player.

I would encourage everyone, not just people at a transition point in their life, to benefit from a life coach or an accountability partner. All of us can benefit from an external structure that can help us or someone who can help speak greatness into us. For example, I started working with Mac for one year while I was still playing. Likewise, I would encourage other professional athletes to have someone they work with outside of the organization to give them unbiased feedback into their lives.

When I was in the NFL, the coaches were concerned with the team as a whole, so although we did get some individualized feedback, they didn't have time to pour into everybody on an in-depth level. That's why I think it's great having personal coaches in your life, whether they be an executive coach, a mindset coach, a performance coach, or whatever you want to call them. There's a significant role for them to fill because they can constantly hold you accountable to fill your mind with the things that will help you.

I realize that not everyone is in the financial position to hire a life coach. However, sometimes an accountability partner can be just as constructive, and all it costs is their time. An accountability partner is someone you check in with regularly, figure once or twice a week, and helps you go over all the goals you have set for yourself. They can be a friend, a mentor, or a relative.

There are also other things you can do to take responsibility for your mind and thoughts. In those situations when you don't have someone who has time to pour into you, you can adapt to your environment and start pouring into yourself. And that can begin with gatekeeping the kind of information you consume. It should all be a deliberate choice, starting with that device you carry around in your pocket.

How to Start Filling Your Mind Intentionally

The same personal devices that can do so much to distract us can also be a powerful tool to take control of your mind. Your phone is a supercomputer with endless possibilities if you know how to use it. I would start with looking at podcasts, videos, and audio or digital books that contain information that uplifts you, positively influences you, and enables you to grow. Any self-development material is outstanding. Fill your mind with it and make it a part of your routine, so one of the first things you are digesting in the morning is information that will get you on the path you want to go. I like books on audio because I can listen to them while doing other things, such as working out, although I understand some people prefer books in print, and I enjoy plenty of those, too.

There were many books I read early on and soaked up like a sponge. I'm still obsessed with soaking up information. I always want to be a super-learner and absorb information and integrate it into my life. There is always so much to learn, such an abundance of information available to practically everyone. You just have to choose.

Choosing one thing eliminates others, so it's best to align your media consumption with your goals systematically. That one hour you are reading or listening to enriching content is an hour you are *not* spending second-guessing yourself or getting your attention sent down a rabbit hole of competing media. Maybe you want to listen to a sermon, a lecture, a documentary, or some other self-development material. Any of that is better than passively scrolling through your social media feeds for an hour.

As Jon Gordon says, "Thoughts are magnetic. What we think about, we attract." That's why it's so important to get in the practice of listening to people you admire and filling your mind with possibility and promise. Your mind thrives on a healthy diet of positivity, growth, and stimulation, just like your body thrives with healthy food and exercise.

If you're thinking about 6,000 thoughts a day, wouldn't you rather you be in control of them and have your thoughts working for you? Unfortunately, most people remain on autopilot, and the majority of those thoughts, maybe as high as 90%, are negative or unhelpful. There is untold power to inverting that number so that at least 90% of your thoughts are positive, intentional, and helping you along your path.

It requires you to choose to be in the present, be awake, and choose content and thoughts every moment that help you forward.

Don't Limit Yourself

You don't have to limit yourself to an ordinary life. The question is, where do you want to go? The information available to you is unlimited. All the pieces are out there for you to put together.

You are not limited, even if you grew up in very challenging circumstances. Maybe you had financial struggles in your family growing up, maybe there were addiction issues in your family, or perhaps you grew up with abuse or discrimination. Maybe, like so many people, you came from a broken home or were a child of divorce. Those pervasive elements become part of the story you tell yourself about yourself. Then that story seems like an irreversible fact about your future. There is power in absorbing different content, which shows you a different story, a new story that can become yours.

You read a book or hear a speech. You consume information that reverses a story, or someone speaks confidence into you. The power of words to me is truly remarkable. That's why I admire people who are intentional about how they speak to others because they could change someone's life by one compliment, one encouragement, one piece of positive information that the other person may never have heard before. It can flip a person's story, overturning a bucket of false assumptions and self-limiting beliefs. It is amazing to me how many of the high-achieving guests on my podcast can pinpoint an occasion in their life when someone gave them the confidence to succeed at a high level based on words spoken to them.

You can also start with other people in your life. You can always request people to give you some time to offer their advice. You'd be surprised how many people want to help. Outside of your personal network, there are plentiful options to learn from some of the greats.

There are free and low-cost seminars, online courses, books, training programs, certificate programs, and events. I encourage everyone to shop around for what works for them—there are dozens of powerful speakers from all walks of life aligned with your goals who want to deliver information that you can use to grow. It's part of their mission to help you. You just have to connect with them and their content.

You can access incredible content through digital books and print, the library, or through YouTube or the internet—never in history has so much information been freely available. The only thing putting limits on what you can learn is you. Your mind is hungry for the fuel to make it grow.

All the most high-performance and self-actualized people I know absorb self-development content constantly. It comes naturally to them. You can do the same. Fill your mind with the best and most helpful content you can find, and watch as the things you focus on start showing up in your life.

Key Takeaways

Here are the key takeaways to filling your mind with what you want to show up in your life:

- What you think, you become.
- Your thoughts become your behavior, your behavior becomes your actions, your actions become your future.
- There are significant obstacles to controlling your thoughts.
- One obstacle is the sheer number of thoughts you have each day, between 6,000 by some estimates and other estimates at 60,000.
- Another obstacle is self-limiting beliefs and negative self-talk.
- Yet another obstacle is the constant media bombardment that competes for your mind's attention.

- Despite it all, you still have the power to choose your thoughts.

- You can control your thoughts with practice as part of your morning and daily routine.

- You have a choice in what media you consume and what you believe.

- There are nearly unlimited options for self-development—you can pick and choose what you wish to learn over multiple platforms.

- You can replace negative habits with positive ones.

- You don't have to limit yourself—you can always change the story you believe in.

- The more you fill your mind with positivity and growth-related material, the more it will show up in your life.

11 Examine the People You Are Spending the Most Time With

As iron sharpens iron, so one person sharpens another.

—Proverbs 27:17

Just as you have to be intentional about what you are consuming and what you are thinking, you also must be mindful of the people you are spending the most time with. All that time you spend with them makes an impact. Over time, you become more and more like the people you spend the most time with. It's inevitable.

So then the questions become, "How are you being guided and influenced by the people with whom you spend the most time? Are they making you better? The same? Or worse?"

Most people would rather keep things the same than risk uncomfortable change. However, when we take that risk and consciously curate the people who can add the most value to our lives, we enter into a community that uplifts each other and supports us to succeed in ways we may not have thought possible.

The Profound Influence of the People You Spend the Most Time With

The late Jim Rohn, famous entrepreneur, author, and speaker, once said, "You are the average of the five people you spend the most time with." Though that was an opinion and wasn't a scientific assessment, it's still a quote that you will see popping up in business and psychology articles to this day. As the decades pass since he originally made that statement, evidence has accumulated that he may have been right. Some people have even taken it further financially, saying that, over time, you'll earn within either $2,500 or $5,000 of the average income of the five people you spend the most time with.

I don't think anybody doubts the value of having close friends in our lives or having regular social interaction. It's part of what it means to be human. However, with that engagement and the social need for interaction also comes influence. You are influencing your circle of friends, and they are influencing you. Some researchers call this a network; others compare it to an ecosystem. The gist is that you are all influencing each other inside the circle for better or worse. And that influence can have surprising impacts on your psychology.

Just on the health front, your friends' attitudes toward healthy habits are likely to influence your own. If they eat healthy food, chances are you will as well. If they exercise regularly, you probably will too. But the same goes toward unhealthy habits, which can gang up on you down the road.

On that front, strong-willed friends might rub off on you and help you conquer habits that you wish to replace. This is part of the idea of having an accountability partner, someone to help you stick to your goals and manage your self-control. Seeking out people with strengths in areas where you have a weakness is a great way to enrich your team of friends. In short, they help round you out.

Together, a circle of friends with different strengths and backgrounds can be an ideal group to help each other earn and maintain success in all the buckets of their life. One metaphor that I use to visualize a great circle of friends is a high-performing football team.

Even though a football team is composed of all athletes at the top of their game, they do not all look similar to each other. They all have remarkably different yet complementary skill sets based on their position. For example, if you ever look at a kicker, you might think, "Wait? That guy plays the same sport?" Because the kicker doesn't look like a 330-pound offensive lineman. But you need that kicker—a lot of games come down to the kicker, and many games are decided with three points or less.

Another example is the long snapper—all he does is throw the ball 15 yards on punts and 8 yards on field goals back between his legs, and often he doesn't look like the prototypical football player, either. Likewise, wide receivers don't look like offensive linemen. They all have different skill sets, but you need all of them to form a championship football team.

A championship football team doesn't have all guys who are just perfectly built at six foot five and 250 pounds to play any position. It's not the same as other sports. For example, in basketball, you could have five Kevin Durants on a team and win a championship. In football, arguably the best player of all time is Tom Brady, but you couldn't have 22 of him and win a championship. As much as I love Tom Brady, he's not tackling anybody, and he's not blocking anybody. He's not very fast, either.

So, that being said, your group of friends, the people you surround yourself with most, need to be well-rounded because God gives us all individual strengths, weaknesses, and passions. Someone who's passionate about health and wellness, or finance, or what have you may be able to help round you out where God may not have blessed you in your life. You need many different types to make it work.

Your Profound Influence on Others

Friendship is a two-way street—it's not just their influence on you; it's your influence on them. There's a lot of potential power and responsibility going both ways on that, so it's valuable to start thinking of your friendships in much larger terms and what *you* are bringing to the table for others.

Bill Carmody, founder and CEO of Trepoint, had a lot to say about personal influence in an article he wrote in 2016 for *Inc.* entitled "You Are an Influencer: Here's How to Become an Even More Powerful Influencer." He compares the environment of everyone with whom you interact as an ecosystem—an inherently interconnected little universe:

> Every day you are influencing and being influenced by those with whom you surround yourself. Your friends, family, colleagues, employees, clients, and partners make up an ecosystem where you play a vital role. Often you're not even aware of just how much you influence those around you. . . . That's why influence is so important. Every action you take, every word you say and even the body language you unconsciously use tells those around you how you feel and what you want. Often, if you aren't living in a beautiful state, you're negatively influencing people in ways you don't intend.

Carmody makes an excellent point—your energy and attitude project an influence at all times. Your mood and behavior can influence the weather of the entire room. Have you ever experienced a whole group of people perking up their energy when a positive person comes in? The expression "they light up a room" is perfect because that's what it feels like. Conversely, sometimes everyone is having a great time until a certain someone with a bad mood or toxic attitude enters the room, dragging down or diminishing the energy of others. It can feel like a storm or a hurricane, and the very air feels different.

Now, I want to clarify that I think it's okay to have a bad day and feel any number of unpleasant feelings ranging from anger to sadness and everything in between. However, I think it's important not to let those feelings set your default attitude and expectations over the long term. It hurts yourself, and it negatively influences others.

Doug Marrone came to the Bills in 2013 as our head coach. When I would get beat out on the football field, whether in practice or actual games, I had this tendency to rip off my chin strap and throw my helmet on the ground in anger. I honestly wasn't looking for attention. It was just the only thing I had on me that I could possibly throw and try to break.

One time, I remember I was so upset, and I had just thrown my helmet again, and Doug Marrone came up to me after practice and grabbed me. He said, "Hey, I can't have you throwing your helmet anymore like that."

And I said, "I know, I know, but I'm able to kind of snap back into it and regroup before the next play."

I'll never forget what he said next.

He said, "I know, but your energy is affecting everybody else. You got to be careful because you're one of the leaders of our football team. You're one of our captains. We can't have our captain doing that kind of stuff, especially during a game, but even in practice."

And that's when I finally got it. It wasn't just about me or how I was feeling. I had to worry about the team around me and what impact these little storms would have on the rest of them.

Eventually, I began to have more confidence as a person. That confidence was a combination of maturity and devotion to my faith. Leslie commented on it first. She said that since I was on my faith journey, she noticed that my temper had almost completely subsided, especially at home.

I was also proactive and wanted to be more mindful of how my actions affected others. I took it even further when I started meditating and focusing on developing more patience. Eventually, those split-second decisions were affected by what I was filling my mind with in the morning. My patient thoughts became my behaviors, which then became my actions. My actions resulted in a better relationship with my wife and better energy to share with my team.

It's always good to check in and ask yourself these questions:

- How are my thoughts affecting my behavior?
- How is my behavior affecting my actions?
- How are my actions affecting those around me?

Spend Time with People You Can Learn From

While I was still playing for the Bills, the five people I spent the most time with (outside of Leslie) were all members of my team. So if you're the average of the five people you spend the most time with, I was the average of five professional football players. Now, everyone was different. Some guys were partiers, and others took it more seriously. There were Christians and non-Christians, and every type of person under the sun. There are so many different sects within a football team.

I've always tried to gravitate toward people who are one step ahead of me regarding where I'm trying to get to in life. No one ever told me that the best advice for a rookie is to find a veteran player and model what they do because they're the veteran. That just seemed like common sense to me. Find a Pro Bowl player or guy who's won the Super Bowl, and see how that person operates. Look at what they're modeling for you, and follow suit. I've ingrained that in myself because I always wanted to reach the top of my profession.

While I was still in college and highly focused on being NFL-bound, my biggest influences were already in the NFL. Some guys had a massive impact on me when I got to college. There was a guy named Jason Spitz who ended up playing for the Packers. There was another guy named Travis Leffew. They were older offensive linemen, and I tried to act, play, and train as they did.

One of the mentors I learned from early on was a guy who played center, my eventual position, when I first joined the Bills. His name was Geoff Hangartner. He was a custom-made mentor for me because he had already played for four years in the NFL, and he had just signed his second contract. So those were both things that I envisioned for myself. I watched him very closely and tried to absorb how he worked.

I had the opportunity to see his day-to-day process and how he spent time outside of the facility. I saw how he prepared for games, which was rigorous. We were polar opposites in our demeanor on the football field, which worked out well early in my career. As I said, I was a hothead and pretty wild on the football field. By contrast, Geoff was cerebral and exceptionally calm. I've never quite approached Geoff Hangartner's advanced level of calmness, but I found myself having more and more of his kind of demeanor as my career went on. Geoff always treated me like a buddy, even as a rookie, which I'll appreciate for the rest of my life.

Another guy I learned a lot from on my team was the best player on the Bills throughout my entire career. His name is Kyle Williams, and he's a multitime Pro Bowler. He now has five kids, but he had two when we lived right next door to each other. We shared a wall of a two-unit townhouse.

I got to observe Kyle on a day-to-day basis. He's one of the hardest workers I've ever been around in my life, one of the toughest and smartest football players. He's quick, athletic, smart, strong, mean, and an all-around excellent football player. And I got to see how he treated his wife (like gold) and how he approached his faith walk. And I got to see him be a devoted and loving dad. So for me, aligning myself with people like Kyle and following his every move, and being able to see how he operated was extremely valuable for me throughout my entire nine-year NFL career. Kyle entered the league three years before me, and I got to see him the whole way.

Toward the end of my career, I spent the most time with Richie Incognito in the locker room. I never made a Pro Bowl prior to playing with Richie (although I was an alternate a few times), and I believe that being around Richie helped lead me to that. He had been a Pro Bowler in the past, and I got to see his approach to preparing for the game and also recovering after the game—he was an elite at both. Richie had this intense dedication to training and investing in his body through massage therapy, fly-in special physical trainers, whatever it may be. He also raised my play on the field because a center relies so heavily on his guards playing next to him, and he was as good as it gets on the field. If I were still playing for the Bills and moving forward, Richie would have had a tremendous impact. I would have kept emulating that regimen he brought when he came to the Bills.

There were so many incredible people like Geoff, Kyle, and Richie whom I learned from while playing. Yet, at the end of the day, you're still hanging out with pro-football players and coaches who are at the top of their profession. My team had a tremendous influence on me. When you have that kind of infrastructure around you, your average is going to be pretty strong—leaving that group when I had to retire presented some loss and challenges in terms of my circle of friends.

I had to leave this bubble of high performers. And I had to ask myself, "Who am I going to be spending the most time around?"

When I transitioned out of football and started on a new personal development journey, I had a lot of conversations with people who were further along on their paths than I was. They all warned me that I would be spending a lot of time around non-football players, so it was imperative to be intentional about my relationships. I needed to be highly intentional about how I spent my time and who I spent it with.

I spend time with a solid group of buddies of high character in Louisville who round me out well. Most of them attend my Thursday morning men's group each week. A lot of them like to play golf. They are all career-driven and successful in their own right. All of their incomes are different. And one of the most important things to me is that they're great husbands, exceptional dads, and portray a positive attitude. I like to surround myself with funny, competitive, and intelligent people, and they certainly fit the bill.

I've truly been blessed with a group of friends who add value to Leslie's and my life. When you have that, it's a great find.

Find Groups to Learn from Others at an Advanced Level

My podcast has been an incredible learning experience. Learning the art of conversation at a deeper level and becoming better at my interviewing skills are of value. More important, I've learned so much from all the wisdom I've received from guests. People I admire from all walks of life have shared stories about what makes them tick and how they got to be where they are now. It's been an inspiration to me, and I'm so happy that I've been able to build some meaningful friendships out of this experience as well.

Each year, I put together an advisory board of five or six people to help me with strategic vision and long- and short-term goals. Lately, many of them are people I met through my podcast. I may have considered many of them out of my league in the past because of their incredible influence and reach. They are a bunch of heavy-hitters in speaking, writing, digital content, financial prowess, and podcasts. I was completely humbled and blown away they were making time to help me.

I didn't think I could get some of these high-profile guys to volunteer some of their time on my behalf, but I just asked, and they said yes. That's something I think everyone should remember—it never hurts to ask. There are amazing people everywhere with a servant's heart and who are looking for opportunities to help and pay it forward. With a little effort, you can connect with people who believe in your potential.

When I first started using an advisory board after I had retired from the NFL, they helped me narrow my focus on all the things I was trying to do. It's kind of comical how many things I was involved with, far too many to be sustainable. I told them about my foundation boards, charities, various broadcast gigs, a few of my roles in the church, and so forth. They had excellent clarity on this and suggested that when I found the thing I was most passionate about, I would have to cut most of these activities because my schedule was completely crowded.

This year they've been helping me with many things, including most of my next moves in broadcasting and getting into the world of mindset coaching. One of my advisory board members, Ben Newman, already has a fantastic career with mindset coaching. He is the performance coach for Alabama football, Kansas State football, has multiple NFL player clients, and works with a number of NFL teams. One of my other board members, my friend David Nurse, has worked with 150 NBA players as a mindset and performance coach.

They've blazed this trail before and have given me excellent first steps to take and shown me how to get a running start. In addition, they have given me excellent ideas of what kinds of training, seminars, and certifications I might need and a few organizations that were perfect candidates to start working with as a mindset coach. I have no problem doing a deep dive, and it's so helpful to have knowledgeable people act as guides.

Now, if you just look at it as purely hours spent, my advisory board doesn't consist of people I spend the most time with. However, in terms of focused, high-octane quality time, it's about equal in its influence on me as the people I do spend the most time with. These are the kind of conversations that can change the course of your life in less than an hour.

Case in point, on Thursday mornings, I've been attending a group called "Man Challenge" at our church. It's early, 6 am, so it requires some commitment to go. At one point in my life, I felt like I was wrecking my week to get up for it, but now I'm just used to it. It's a group of men, and they bring in a speaker. We all sit at our individual tables, and then we discuss the message afterward.

We always joke that we're just a bunch of men trying to figure it all out. Yet, since 2012, that group has shaped my life and molded me as much as anybody. That's true even though we're only spending an hour and a half a week together. Over the years, there has been such a draw to join our table because of the impact and the men who have come, that our individual table of up to about 10 has had to be divided about four different times to accommodate everyone. These other Christian men shape you, and our ages at our current table range from the late 20s to mid-60s—you get so much life experience. It's great that it's a bunch of guys who round each other out. We're all there to encourage each other, and we're all we're service-oriented.

This group sharpens me constantly to develop into the Christian man I want to become. I encourage anyone out there to find a group of men or women with whom you can have intentional conversations and not just talk sports and careers. We are often talking about the future and who we're becoming and not obsessed with the past. That's a healthy habit for any group to practice.

My point is I know not everyone has access to a formal advisory board—but you do have access to other genuine and helpful groups of people who can help you fill in the gaps and give you much-needed perspective. You can create groups or join existing groups of people to enhance your learning at a high level.

One of the first questions you can ask yourself is, "What are your goals?" For example, if your goals are to develop yourself spiritually, I would start attending groups in churches or other places of worship, go to services, and get involved with helping the community. If, however, your goals are about physical health and getting into shape, I would join a gym and get involved with a class-based gym, so you're around the same people at the same time each week. Those people can positively influence you and vice versa. You'll all be on a similar journey together.

Whenever you're mentoring or pouring your energy into someone else, you're rewarded back for that. So remember—if you want to add someone to your group of five or simply need the advice to get to the next step, people are almost always more willing than you think to meet and try to help. It often means more to them to pay it forward than it does to you.

No matter what your goals, you can find a group correlated to those goals, whether it's through social media or any other community resource. You don't have to limit yourself by your recent experience—connecting with others, asking advice, and getting involved with something greater than yourself can help you learn and upgrade yourself at an exponential level.

Moving On and Letting Go

Pastor Keith Craft had a great saying about the length of friendships. He said, "Some friends are in your life for a season, some friends are in your life for a reason, and some friends are with you for a lifetime." I feel like there's so much wisdom in that sentiment. It's okay that some friends are with you for a short period of time, or others you might share a bond with for a particular reason, and then there are those few that you'll know for the rest of your life.

And sometimes, you just have to let people go. I know that's sometimes easier said than done. I'm a people-pleaser at heart, and I would rather try and bring others along with me instead of cutting them out of my life. I have a hard time doing that, but there are people that I've purposely separated myself from or I choose to spend less time with. Sometimes it's just because we're both in different stages of life.

Key Takeaways

Here are the key takeaways from this chapter:

- We are an average of the five people we spend the most time with.
- It's important to ask ourselves these questions:
  - How are we being guided and influenced by our friends?
  - Are they making us better, the same, or worse?

- The people we spend the most time with have a profound impact on us. They influence our health, our finances, our mood, our long-term goals, and overall habits.

- People we spend the most time with can help round out our weaknesses.

- However, people we spend the most time with can also reinforce bad habits.

- We also have a profound influence on people who spend time with us.

- We must take responsibility for how we influence others. Ask yourself:

  ◆ How are my thoughts affecting my behavior?

  ◆ How is my behavior affecting my actions?

  ◆ How are my actions affecting those around me?

- Spend time with people that you can learn from and who have a positive impact on you.

- Seek out groups to supercharge your learning.

- More people are more willing to help than you might think.

- Learn to let go of people who have a negative influence on you.

12 Be Coachable

It's not all about talent. It's about dependability, consistency, being coachable, and understanding what you need to do to improve.

—Bill Belichick

I've been rigorously coached nearly all my life, and it's only until now have I realized how deep of an experience it really is. Coaching is a relationship between you and the coach and between you and the best version of yourself. And it's not a one-way street—the best coach in the world can't do anything if the person working with them doesn't show up and do the work.

Yes, it's work. There's a practice and even an art to being coachable. Whether it's in a professional sport, a business, your life, or any other situation, the coach you are working with can help you reach levels unattainable by yourself. Your future best self is waiting on the other side. However, to receive the proper guidance, you must have a specific set of attitudes and actions, or it won't take.

From my perspective, there are things you need to bring to the table for a coach to help you reach your highest potential.

First, Be Accountable

Accountability is a way to track your integrity and responsibility. It's a way to take a snapshot of where you are now. Are you doing the things you said you would do? Are you tracking your progress with meaningful measurements? If you're not willing to be accountable, then this is where you'd get off the train. Coaching isn't for you, and you'd be on your own.

There's a concept called "radical responsibility," which means taking responsibility for everything in your life. Essentially, you're saying, "If my life is great, it's because of my choices and how I react to circumstances. If it's awful, it's also due to my choices and how I react to circumstances." Such a high level of responsibility is scary for most people because it means if something in your life isn't working, it's nobody's fault but your own. You have to take ownership of the problem and how you react to it, even if it's something you didn't directly control, such as a natural disaster or a scary diagnosis. The scary thing is that means you can't blame anybody or anything else for what's happening. But the fantastic thing is that it also means that if something isn't working, you have the power to change it. By the ways you react and your actions, you can take control.

In the world of football, you are 100% accountable for your performance. What the NFL requires of you is so precise and requires such dedication that coaches and organizations won't let you get away with being sloppy with your technique, effort, or knowing your given assignment on each play—and they have built-in methods to keep you on the right track.

The NFL was on an entirely different level. By the time players get to the NFL, everyone down the line is paid handsomely—so the NFL knows how to leverage that carrot with the appropriate stick when necessary. For example, they created a schedule of extreme fines if you were late to practice or meetings, which was considered one of the worst things you could ever do. It was a $1,700 fine if you were even *one second late* when I was playing for the Bills.

So if you missed a whole day of practice, you might be paying between $10,000 and $15,000 in fines! It wasn't just the money—the embarrassment of getting a late penalty when everyone else showed up on time was just far too much. Guess what? Most people showed up on time.

It didn't stop there. We would weigh ourselves in on Friday mornings—we were required to stay within a specific weight range. Coaches would be there, sitting in on the weigh-in. If we were even one pound over, we were considered overweight. They would charge you $550 a pound for every extra pound and fined that amount every day until your weight was within the correct range.

Another example was the kind of fines you might get for inappropriate behavior on the field during games, for example, if you hit someone's head violently or if you did a block and cut someone's legs out from underneath them. If you got a severe penalty on the field, you know you're going to get an official FedEx envelope at your locker that would charge you an exorbitant fine, depending on the offense. I was the recipient of one of those envelopes once—it was an unintended accident where I cut someone's legs from underneath them in an illegal way during a block. I was able to explain myself and got the fine rescinded.

Naturally, the culture of accountability trickled down to the players who would hold themselves accountable to each other. Of course, we wouldn't send each other threatening FedEx envelopes, but we did develop little systems and rituals to keep each other in check. A prime example was the offensive line on our team.

In virtually every NFL team, the offensive line is generally the closest unit, the ones most in tune with each other. We spend the most time together, so it's almost always the case. The offensive line performs as a single entity. If one of us does poorly in a play, we all look bad. It's never, "Hey, this guy gave up a sack." It's the offensive line that gave up the sack. We're all so close on the line of scrimmage and so physically close in proximity. We would get to be in sync, operating as one entity.

With the Bills, our offensive line had a pot of money we had accumulated at the end of the season from our own little system of fines we would give each other. It was just for fun, and at the end of the season, we would donate half of it to charity, and with the other half, we would take a trip together.

We had this system of dinging each other if someone took a coaching direction too seriously or too personally. They'd get dinged for being too sensitive. We all had the attitude not to be too sensitive because we were all supposed to be easily coachable. Or maybe someone jumped offsides before the play was going. Or perhaps we missed an assignment (an assignment is what you were required to do on a specific play). The team or the league wouldn't fine us, but internally, we would fine ourselves. It looks terrible for everybody if anyone doesn't know what they're supposed to do and starts missing assignments.

They weren't hefty fines—ranging from $5 to $20 per offense. But in the case of the internal fines, it was just an extra layer of accountability. We made it fun, too. Anyone could ding anyone else for an offense, so it kept us on our toes.

I had an old school bell that literally made that ding sound. So I was usually the one that made the ding. I was in charge of funds, too. I would have fun with it—for example, if someone was dinged for being sensitive, and then they claimed they weren't being sensitive, I would say, "You're still being sensitive." And ding him again. And he might say, "Okay, write it up." And then I'd ding him again, and then we'd all laugh.

We had four layers of accountability that committed us to greatness with the league, the Bills, the coaches, and the players. How many of us go through life with zero accountability at all?

The price of entry for greatness at anything, at the very least, is accountability.

Be Willing to Be Uncomfortable

The process of getting better at something is rarely easy. It requires you to go through multiple levels of potential discomfort. One of the first levels of discomfort is simply the realization that you need to improve something. When someone gives us feedback, we may be preconditioned to take it personally—that there's something wrong with us internally; otherwise, we'd be better at whatever it is.

You can't take it personally. Or if you do, you won't last long.

If someone takes the time to coach you or give you valuable feedback, they are on your side. They want you to progress! They see these things you can improve—whether that's on-field performance, your marriage, career, or any other facet of your life. Yes, that's difficult at times because if you're not used to criticism, it's hard to hear about things you could do better. Just remember, it's never a personal attack on you.

Some people spend their whole lives either deflecting criticism or avoiding it. Those people never get very far in any dream they've ever had.

In football, everything was on video. Every single thing was watched afterward on film. So, yes, it's constant criticism, but that's how you get better.

Even with this context and background, I recognize it can be uncomfortable to start an unfamiliar coaching process. When I first started working with Mac and having an accountability partner, I wasn't necessarily used to being coached on certain areas of my life—and a lot of questions were far from comfortable. For example, how are you managing your time? How are you spending the first

30 minutes of your day? Who are you spending the most time with? Yet, it was necessary to push through that discomfort to get to the what's next part of my life.

The best coaches in life push you out of your comfort zone so that you can be your best. Mac does that with me now. Bobby Petrino and Mike Summers did that for me in college. Coach Petrino was our head coach, and Coach Summers was our offensive line coach during my first three years at Louisville. Those were two extremely tough coaches—they were just constantly demanding nothing short of everyday excellence. For the first time in my life, I understood what that tough coaching was.

Don't get me wrong—I had great coaches in high school who pushed us, but they just took it to another level at Louisville. Our strength coach at the time, Jason Veltkamp, pushed us beyond our limits. We would do these drills on Friday mornings. He called them "full metal jackets," a title based on the war movie. It was essentially an hour torture session for us.

Another thing we did was sit in a squat with a giant boulder in our arms. It would be cutting up our forearms and taxing our legs because we couldn't fully stand up. We had all types of drills like that in the full metal jacket, each more punishing than the last. But if you do enough of those in a row, you gain confidence, strength, and grit through that intense coaching. You couldn't do it without them!

On my podcast, I had a fantastic conversation about being uncomfortable with Robert O'Neill, an ex-Navy SEAL known for being on the missions that killed Osama Bin Laden and rescued Captain Phillips (he actually was the one that shot Bin Laden). These days, Robert O'Neill is a motivational speaker and a FOX News contributor. Robert spoke at length about his BUD/S training as a Navy SEAL, a fierce program that makes my full metal jacket drills look tame by comparison.

It is the three-week orientation training to become a Navy SEAL. The first tip about dealing with discomfort was not to think about accomplishing everything at once. Don't think about winning the week; think about winning the day. Or, as he put it, "I've got to make it to breakfast." His instructor told him, "I'll never ask you to do the impossible. I'll ask you to do something very hard, followed by something very hard, followed by something very hard." Take everything one step at a time.

The instructor gave everyone in training his own particular brand of motivation. He said, "You're about to go to war for the first time, and the enemy is all your doubts, all your fears, and everyone you know back home who told you you weren't good enough to do this. Keep your head down, keep moving forward, no matter what, never quit, and you'll be fine." On the same topic, the quote that Robert shared from his instructor that I'll never forget is, "Don't quit now, quit tomorrow. If you keep quitting tomorrow, you can do anything."

How many times have you quit something in life that you now regret? There are so many times people quit in the moment and later wish they didn't. The pain of regret is far greater than the pain of discomfort. So stay with that discomfort and push through.

Practice Humility and Confidence at the Same Time

You need to have a certain amount of humility to be coachable. But then also, you need to have a combination of confidence with your humility to inspire and lead others and make an impact in this world. It's a weird paradox because you need both, yet it has to be the right balance. Too much humility, and you might take things too personally and not be able to execute. But, on the other hand, too much confidence and you become arrogant and unable to receive feedback properly, thus making it so you can never improve.

I think it's one of the biggest challenges to being coachable for some people—the humility that comes with accepting that someone knows more than you. Someone who has been further in life than you. Someone who knows better than you do about a particular situation. Or one of the hardest things about being coachable is that you're going to create new habits. And anytime you're creating new habits, whether that's on the football field or life, you're going to be uncomfortable, and that's not going to be fun.

Michael Jordan, arguably the best overall basketball player of all time, said, "My best skill was that I was coachable. I was a sponge and aggressive to learn." And you could see that right out there on the basketball court. I've read Tim Grover's book, called *Winning*, and he talks a lot about his work with Michael Jordan. It's fascinating, but Michael was always looking for some type of edge to improve. So the guy you would assume would have the confidence that he was already good enough, and maybe he should just keep rolling, actually just wanted to be coached. That's amazing.

That's how you become the greatest of all time and don't fall off at any point and win those championships late in your career. It's by continuing to get better and be coachable versus being unwilling to learn from difficult coachable moments to continue to improve.

Hold Yourself to a Higher Standard by Seeking Coaching

Once you start holding yourself to a higher standard, maybe higher than most, then you've opened the door to ascend to greatness. You might have to ask for help and get lasered-in specific about what kind of feedback you're looking for.

For example, when I went to Louisville, I had never played center. I had only played offensive line for one year in high school—I played tackle. Well, there was an opening at center on our college team. That was the only way I would be able to start as a freshman, so I transitioned to center.

There was only one problem: I had never snapped a football in my life before. My snaps were sporadic because I was just trying to wing it. I just thought you throw a football through your legs, similar to how you would throw a football overhand on any other play, and how hard could that be? That wasn't going to be good enough for the team, and Bobby Petrino noticed right away.

Coach Petrino took me into our weight room and drilled me mercilessly to perfect my snap. He said, "I want every single one to hit me on the belt buckle." In the beginning, I had no accuracy at all. He'd say, "No, this one went left because you're stepping to your left. You need to be able to hit the same spot on your leg with your forearm as you release the ball on every snap to keep it consistent." He worked with me until I mastered that snap.

He essentially taught me how to snap a football in that moment. It was a lot of pressure when you're an 18-year-old kid trying to prove yourself and learn something new. But when he taught me that, even way later, when I was 32 years old playing in the National Football League, I could revisit that coaching. If my snaps got a little sporadic or off-center, I would think back and make all the slight adjustments he taught me.

When you show you are coachable, you are showing coaches that you are trustworthy. Coaches in sports need trust. When you do what you say you're going to do, what you trained yourself to do, you also build trust and confidence in yourself. Business leaders are looking for that same trust as well.

Post-career, of course, I still craved that extra coaching. I wanted mentors and accountability partners in the areas of life I was trying to succeed in. It was so confusing at first in broadcasting. Not getting the feedback, I had no idea how well I was doing.

For example, there are a lot of times in broadcasting when I would be working with a different producer or a different director every week. There's no consistent curriculum in the broadcast world.

I discovered quickly that there are broadcast coaches out there that could help me. For example, I worked with Gerry Matalon, who helped me prep for my interviews with ESPN and Fox. However, beyond that, I had to learn on the fly and had to seek my own feedback actively.

Not having the feedback I needed made it difficult to understand where I stood. If you don't have metrics, how can you improve? Thankfully, some generous veterans of the business showed me some of the ropes. For instance, Adam Bryant was a producer on most of the broadcasts my first year with ESPN and ACC Network. In the first game of the season, we had NC State, so I interviewed their head coach, Dave Doren, after the game. I made a total rookie mistake: I faced the camera, not him.

I was so used to facing the camera and, I'll never forget it; Adam said, "No one wants to see you. They want to see the coach, and you line him perfectly up with the camera. You have to stand to the side and get out of the way. If they want to include you in the shot, they will." I had never been told that before. I just had walked up and put my arm around him and conducted the interview (during the pandemic, I also quickly learned you never put your arm around the coach either). Adam gave me a few pointers, and I loved it. And now, for the rest of my life, I know exactly how I'm supposed to line up a coach in an interview.

I had to learn to find those coachable little moments so I could truly learn on the fly. It's not like the football field where you are taught everything, and at training camp, you iron out any of the wrinkles before the season gets going.

Push Your Limits

When confronted with extreme adversity, we have a natural tendency in our lives to quit far too soon. We think we're running on empty when we actually have a reserve tank that goes untapped. So when you hit those extremely uncomfortable moments in life, your heart races, you start sweating, and you pull back in those moments. That's where having a coach who can push you through those exact moments can be so valuable.

My advisory board often serves that purpose for me. All of the board members are such high performers and much farther along on the journey than I am, so I value their input tremendously. They really put me in the hot seat. I have to wear a dark shirt to my advisory board calls and meetings because I know that I will sweat buckets. That gives you an idea of how valuable those meetings are to me and the level of coaching I receive!

I was so glad Mac encouraged me to get out of my comfort zone on my podcast. He pointed out that during quarantine, everybody would be home now. Four people on that advisory board were guests on my podcast, including bestselling author Jon Gordon. I've developed a relationship with all of them. It was by reaching out last year and trying to align myself with people just like them. I was worried about reaching out. I thought they might think it was a dumb idea. I even thought they might laugh at me. Well, now I have all four guys in my corner, and it's a powerful alignment for the type of work I'm getting into. They were a big reason why I even had the courage to write this book.

I think it's not only a great idea but necessary to build discomfort into your routine, so you're pushing yourself past that discomfort every day. The mental and physical conditioning you build up makes you more resilient to unexpected challenges that pop up when you least expect them. Even if it's just increasing your reps or time exercising—the idea is that you are constantly being challenged by your physical limits. It's great for your confidence at facing obstacles—subconsciously, you start to see challenges as something you can easily conquer. After all—you deal with them every day!

Pivot and Be Flexible

I had to learn how to pivot and be flexible long before my career-ending injury. One of the hardest things about playing for the Bills when I did was that we went through seven different head coaches in nine years and five completely different staffs, teaching separate and distinct techniques. Everyone has different expectations of you. If you wanted to keep your job, you had to learn the new way without grumbling or complaining about it.

That's a great microcosm of life in general. You constantly have to learn new techniques and their nuances as life around you changes. Sometimes the old ways don't work, and even if we know they don't work, it's hard to let go of them because we've become accustomed to a particular way of doing things.

Back then, maybe for a casual football fan, they might not have seen a whole lot of change in the way I was playing or the plays we were running. But there were all these little different skills we had to keep learning, keep picking up constantly. One of the reasons why I was able to stick around with the Bills for nine years (and was signed through 11 years) was because I was willing to be coachable and adaptable as we switched schemes from more of a power-based offense to more of a finessed wide zone scheme offense. I was ready to put in the time to learn those new skills. I would watch film of where the offensive coordinator was previously and watch his center execute in certain situations so I could try and emulate him—all so I could keep my job with the Bills.

Look at what's happened in the past few years in the world of business. After COVID-19 hit, everything changed. It's a struggle to keep up with the learning curve on technology, and the pandemic only accelerated it. Five years ago, the business world looked very different. Who would have thought that most business meetings would be run through Zoom?

Let me tell you about my friend Dan Oliver, a Louisville-based entrepreneur who had a rapid rise to success. Dan told me his story on my podcast, and his journey is a perfect example of how to pivot and be flexible. Dan lost his regular day job and started working at a bar at age 37. Sometimes as part of his job, he would work in the kitchen, and he started making a chicken dish with a custom blend of spices and seasoning that he made himself. Customers raved about the seasoning. So Dan started going to trade shows, state fairs, and barbecue festivals, marketing his "Dan-O's" seasoning directly. With his grassroots marketing efforts, he was making low six figures in addition to his job as a bartender.

Then the pandemic hit, and Dan lost all that extra income. Initially, he thought this was another failed dream, and he'd just have to move on. But before he threw in the towel, he listened to an entrepreneurial podcast, "The Gary Vee Audio Experience." In it, Gary Vee strongly suggested that if you're a small business and you're not marketing on Tik-Tok, the social media video site, then you were missing out on a lot of revenue.

Dan took Gary Vee's advice seriously and started making some moves. He hired a marketing company to put up some videos on Tik Tok. And since he couldn't pay them their fee directly, he offered to give them half of the company in exchange for doing all his marketing. It was a bold move, with no guarantee of success.

The marketing company ended up building him a following of more than 2 million fans on Tik Tok, rapidly developing a huge social media presence. Now they are on pace to make well into eight figures in revenue. Inspired by his story, I invested in the company as well!

Dan pivoted hard when he realized he couldn't do any marketing at live events anymore during the pandemic, so he went online. So here's a guy who has no tech background at all, who wasn't even that social media savvy, who found a way to pivot, and who is likely going to create generational income and wealth for his family.

If you think about it, it's multiple pivots. He pivoted once being fired from his job and working as a bartender, twice by creating a new seasoning and marketing it at live events, and three times when the pandemic hit, and he was forced to go online to sell his seasoning. Kind of like a coach that keeps throwing surprise drills at you, the universe threw him curveballs. He was able to adapt and thrive.

The better you can flow with change, the more you allow yourself to be coached in real time by the events around you.

The Best Coaching Is Ongoing

Jordan Montgomery said that there was a difference between being teachable and coachable. If you're teachable, you're willing to listen to what is being taught to you. Being coachable means that you are eager to put that teaching into practice, and you show the coach or tell them how you implemented their coaching. You're bringing the learning they gave you back to them, and this completes the circle.

I have had the pleasure of getting connected to some of the top coaches in the world, whether that is in sports or life optimization. On my podcast, some of these incredible coaches on the sports side include Sean McDermott, Scott Satterfield, Dabo Swinney, Mike Vrable, Leslie Frazier, and Chris Mack. On life coaching, mindset coaching, and life optimization, I've hosted Craig Ballantyne, Ed Mylett, David Nurse, Jon Gordon, Ben Newman, Greg Taylor, Jason Selk, Michael Gervais, and Jordan Montgomery . . . just to name a few.

I have used my podcast to essentially be a one-hour coaching session a week for my listeners and me. Some of them are packed with so much golden information from my guests that when I relisten to them, I find myself hitting the rewind 30 seconds button constantly just to absorb and pick up all the nuggets of what they are saying.

I'm striving to integrate all the wisdom I pick up, and I stay in touch as much as I can to let these great coaches know how they've affected me. You can honor the coaches in your life by picking up what they've taught you, putting it into practice, and sharing with them the impact it has made. That helps fulfill them and be aware of the positive effects they are having on the world through you. As a people, we are blessed with each other to help each other. Proverbs 11:14 says, "Where there is no guidance, a people falls, but in an abundance of counselors there is safety."

It's such a powerful relationship in sports, this coaching cycle, where they teach you and observe you, and then you put it into practice, and they teach you again. It's a constant give-and-take. So when you're lucky to have effective coaches in your life, you want to honor that process and relationship as much as possible.

Key Takeaways

Here are the key takeaways from this chapter. To be coachable, you have to bring several qualities to the table:

- You must be accountable, first and foremost.
  - Being accountable means you do what you say you are going to do.
  - Being accountable also means you take full responsibility for your actions.
- You must be willing to be uncomfortable.
  - If you can't get out of your comfort zone, you can't grow.
  - Discomfort is natural when learning new habits.

- You must practice humility and confidence at the same time.
  - Even the greatest players in the world know there is room for improvement.
  - Those who remain humble and coachable often rise to the top.
- You must push your limits by seeking coaching.
  - Great coaches often push you past what you thought your limits were.
  - Seek meaningful metrics and feedback so you can track your improvement.
- Pivot and be flexible—life is constantly changing, and you need to keep up.
- The best coaching is ongoing.
  - Being teachable is learning something once.
  - Being coachable is taking what you've learned back to the coach to develop it further.

13 Control What You Can Control

Champions do not become champions when they win the event, but in the hours, weeks, months, and years they spend preparing for it. The victorious performance itself is merely the demonstration of their championship character.

—Alan Armstrong

When I was just coming out of college and preparing for the NFL draft, the sports pundits-that-be gave me a label that I wasn't sure how to feel about. The consensus was that I was the most "prepared" player in the draft. Not the strongest, or the fastest, although God did not slight me on my physical gifts. Nor was I the toughest or even the most experienced. Simply the most prepared. But the way they said "the most prepared" sounded like a compliment. So, at first, why did it not feel like it?

Maybe the most straightforward answer is that preparation isn't glamorous. It isn't flashy, nor is it immediately visible. Out there on the field, you measure the quality of the performance on each play, but you can't see the hundreds and thousands of hours that went into it. Of course, the fans see the game, but that's only 3% of our work as players. The rest of it is all in preparation. As legendary college coach Dabo Swinney says, "All the great players love the preparation."

As an offensive lineman, if the defense is moving in and blitzing and you can stay under control, you generally anticipate what they're doing. So it's not all reactionary. A lot of it is anticipation, and that comes from film study and being able to recognize with your eyes in a concise amount of time what's about to happen. Because you've seen it before. That's part of the reason I started using visualization techniques in the NFL.

However, in college, I wasn't using visualization techniques just yet. I was simply just watching as much film as possible to understand what the defense was doing. With all that research, I could anticipate what they were doing to allow myself to play a more dynamic game. When you know the plays, time has the illusion of slowing down, and it made the game easier for me.

I went to the NFL Scouting Combine prepared—I lived in California for over three months to train specifically for the NFL Combine. I was told by Rick Dennison, who was the offensive line coach for the Broncos, that I was the only player he ever scouted that got over 30 bench press reps at 225 pounds, over 30 inches on the vertical leap, and over a 30 score on the Wonderlic Cognitive Ability Test. Apparently, that's a unique combination of strength, athleticism, and mental dexterity, and that came with the massive amount of preparation prior to the combine. Similar to the actual game, people didn't see the hard work in California. They simply saw the results when it was time to perform in Indianapolis at the Combine.

That's likely what the coaches and commentators spotted in me when I was drafted—that I was willing to take it to the next level in my off-field preparation. I watched the most film and studied my opponents the most. I trained my body in college with discipline and focus, gaining massive strength in a truncated time. Once I understood that they could see all that preparation in how I was playing, my mind shifted, and I started to take it as the honorable commendation that it was.

These days I still try to be as prepared as possible. Everything I do is a preparation process, seemingly mundane process goals that make up a more significant overall product goal. For example, I prepare my clothes the night before. I plan my meals and prep my supplements for the week, and I prepare with my morning routine for the day. I prepare my mind with my gratitude journal and my memory verses. I prepare for Grace's future boyfriends by being the best example of a man I can be (and also try to keep an intimidating physique). In everything, I prepare as I did on the football field. I'm not alone—the best of the best prepare their mind and body, and they do it every day.

This entire book is about preparation, controlling the elements you can control every day. Every chapter contains a vital aspect to preparation.

However—you have to *want* to.

Intentionality and Self-Discipline: How Badly Do You Want It?

The hardest part about preparing is that it takes intentionality and willingness to change. And let's admit it, change is hard for a lot of people, including myself. You win success on a daily basis—as Jeff Olson says in *The Slight Edge*, it's what you do every day. Once you can create the proper habits that prepare you every day for success, you can evolve to where it doesn't take the same kind of willpower each day to prepare. It becomes second nature.

Pastor Keith Craft believes self-discipline is the key to success. "Everything starts with self-discipline," Craft said. "Self-discipline leads to self-discovery. Discovery leads to gifts; gifts lead to talent, talent to ability, and ability to competency."

I have come to peace with my football career ending because I know I did every possible thing off-field to prepare and enhance my performance. Knowing what I know now, maybe I would have shifted a few things here or there. But at the time, there wasn't a single effort

I left on the table. I can't imagine working harder than I did. Yet, I know some athletes even go a step beyond.

Mindset coach Collin Henderson touched on the no-regrets point when he was a guest on my podcast. Collin said the athletes who give it their all are the ones who have an easier time transitioning out of sports. It's the ones who may have held back who have regrets and ongoing disappointment. As Collin put it, those athletes might think, "I could have worked harder. I could have not gone and partied all night. I could have studied more of my playbook. I could have worked harder in the weight room. Those guys have a hard time moving forward."

The work-life balance isn't easy in football, with hundreds of hours of preparation leading to only a few moments of high-stakes game play per game. Those moments are hard-won.

It's weird to think about, but there are only minutes of actual game play, but a football game lasts for hours. Some people might say that football players are paid way too much money to play for three hours on Sunday. But it's not three hours—it's way more than that. At first, I can see why someone might think that. An average NFL play lasts six seconds for the offensive unit in football. The last year I played, I had about 65 snaps a game. So I'd be playing in a game between the whistles—I'd be doing my game-day job for a total of an hour or hour and 44 minutes for the entire season.

However, that's for a season of being adequately prepared, which takes hundreds of hours of practice, no matter if it just breaks down to a few minutes in an actual game. So, six and a half minutes is what I was judged for on a Sunday. That's what it all comes down to. But throughout that week, I'm judged by how much preparation I can do to make those short minutes my best yet! It is no different from how you prepare for other things in life—hundreds of hours of preparation for high-performance moments that make a difference.

Here's the hard truth, too. We all have every morning and every day to prepare, either intentionally or unintentionally. If you're unintentional and undisciplined about how you prepare, or if you're not preparing at all, then you're going to have an unintended and unprepared future. Trust me—you don't want that. Successful people get intentional about what they're preparing, get disciplined about it, and put in the hard work. There is simply no substitute for solid preparation.

Consistency Comes from Preparation

As an athlete, I know if I practice the same drill over and over again, eventually, I stop thinking about it. The routine is in my body. Like when Bobby Petrino taught me how to snap correctly, I have since snapped the ball so many times that I'll never forget it. It's in my muscle memory.

Similarly, when you are the most prepared, the most practiced at whatever you are doing, you don't have to think about technique so much. Instead, your mind and your body simply know what to do. As a result, you develop a level of consistency that is only possible with diligent experience, drilling, and discipline. When that happens, you can focus on the task at hand without consciously worrying about your technique or skill. Essentially, you can perform at an optimal level.

Michael Gervais was a guest on my podcast, and he had some fascinating things to say about optimal performance. Michael is a high-performance psychologist who works in the trenches of high-stakes environments with some of the best in the world, including Olympians, Fortune 100 CEOs, world-class athletes, and internationally acclaimed artists and musicians. On a scale of 1 to 10, he explained that everyone performs optimally between a

4 and a 6 in intensity. Anything higher than 6, and you're going to play outside of your ideal state potentially. For example, it might be too much passion or anger taking you out of your technique and fundamentals.

It takes a foundation of solid preparation and practice in the hundreds of hours before the game to stay in that optimal sweet spot between 4 and 6. At that point, you've firmly established the fundamentals in your body and mind. You can put your intensity right in the middle of that sweet spot, not needing to go maximum intensity because you have your technique and fundamentals solid.

I do believe that technique and fundamentals are in service to a long-term vision. Yet, on a day-to-day level, it's essential to focus on your process goals, the things you need to do every day to get to that vision. You need to break it down and do those steps to make your day-to-day consistent so that your performance on the other end will end up being consistent, too.

Let's get back to Jason Selk's process goals. A vision and plan are great, but you're going to be completely overwhelmed if you're always just thinking about three to five years out. Eventually, if you're like me, you're thinking, "I'm too far away, and it's too much time." Instead, think, "What could I keep doing every single day to get you there? What's my 1% each day? What's my 20% over a year?" Whatever you're tracking, how are you getting to that every day?

The world of sports is such a great place to see the fundamentals of process goals and consistency physicalized right in front of you. You can't deny the performance statistics of incredible players. Tiger Woods is a perfect example, a man who practiced relentlessly every day on both his short and long games. Between 2002 and 2005, Tiger Woods faced 1,540 putts from three feet—and made 1,536 of them. If you can make the three-foot putts in your life, over and over with consistency, that can almost always take you further than occasionally making the highlight shot where you focused all your energy.

Preparation leads to consistency. Consistency is practiced on the day-to-day with incremental improvement. Consistency over the long term wins.

Be a Champion for Your High Standards of Performance

One of the elements you can control is the standard you set for yourself and keeping yourself on task to perform at that standard. No one maintains your standards but you. Your execution level will be naturally high once you have prepared for thousands of hours at any charge in any profession. Anything less than that, and you're playing way below your potential, not to the standard it should be.

I say this because low effort should never be a reason why you fail at something. If it is, then you have no one to blame but yourself. No one controls your effort but you. An optimal effort performance does not guarantee success, but a low effort performance pretty much guarantees failure.

One great example to illustrate the point is Jerry Rice, widely regarded as one of the top receivers of all time. He became one of the best receivers ever despite not having nearly as many physical gifts as so many others who played the position. He became the best because his work ethic was legendary. Jerry Rice once said, "Today I will do what others won't, so tomorrow I will do what others can't."

Until my last year in the NFL, the final game of the season was pretty much irrelevant. Whether we won or lost, it did not affect whether the Bills were going to the playoffs—and those were the games that were tough to get excited for. The way the NFL draft works, where it's simply slated, the teams with the worst record at the end of the season get the better draft picks for the next season. And so, often, some people in the regime don't even want you to win.

I believe you have to play to your personal standard no matter what. I would constantly preach to the offensive line: "Hey, we're judged by how all five of us play today. If one guy gives up two sacks because he's going to be lazy today, then the whole offensive line gave up two sacks today." And I would say, "Look, we have to play to our standard today. It does not matter what's going on around us. We want to keep our jobs, and we all still want to be a part of this organization. So we need to play to our standard."

Playing to our high standard wasn't always easy, especially when the high-stakes emotions weren't there because we knew we weren't making it to the playoffs, no matter what happened in that particular game. Our emotions were hurt because we didn't achieve the goals we set out to accomplish that year. But, all of those hurt feelings didn't matter—we would be betraying ourselves if we didn't push through to play to our particular standard (caffeine can help in these instances).

Keeping and maintaining your standard requires you to live in that uncomfortable place sometimes, where you are tired or in pain, or you don't feel like it. Remember when I mentioned in Chapter 12 that you need to be willing to be uncomfortable if you want to be coachable? Your standard is that high coachable level you've trained yourself to reach. Don't ever betray all those hundreds of hours of work, your routine, and your core values just because it feels like it's too hard or you're not "feeling it."

Even if, at times, I feel like doing other things, I keep that personal standard because I don't want to go backward in life.

With Great Preparation Comes Great Confidence

For me, most of the confidence in my life comes from preparation— and that bleeds into everything. That's why all the chapters in this book lead back to preparation. Everything, absolutely everything, leads back to preparation.

If I didn't have the confidence I built from preparation, I would be an anxious wreck heading into a football game, knowing that they could throw something at me. If we could have won the game instead of lost if I had prepared better—that would just eat me up.

There are maybe, on average, about 50 plays on our call sheet for the offensive coordinator to call in a football game. You have to know those 50 plays against so many various defenses and understand them all. That's where it becomes crucial to understand concepts in football as opposed to just straight memorizing. You can see how one play relates to another, for example, concept A is very similar to concept B. I could relate it to that, and then we can block it or throw these routes against these defenses. It would work. Each play will have its different variations depending on what was going on right then.

If you're a quarterback and get up to the line of scrimmage, you could have four receivers going out on a pass route. That could look like four different plays to the crowd. It could look like a deep shot down the sideline or like a check down to the running back. Much of that's dictated by what the defense gives you, which is honestly no different than circumstances that life throws at you.

You think you might know the play because you're so prepared, but you might have to improvise. You're ready and confident to hit that home run throw deep down the field, but sometimes, it's just a check down to the running back. A short little pass that keeps the momentum going on a drive is comparable to short steps that keep the momentum going in your life. Sometimes that's all you get that day. You metaphorically moved the ball a little further down the field.

The more prepared you go into the game, the more muscle memory you've created, and you're not thinking about your technique, so you can better adapt to the defense moving before the snap and what the defense is going to do. But if you're worried about "What foot do I step with first on this play? Oh, am I going to use my left hand or right hand to engage contact?" If you're worried about all those things, you can't possibly be concerned with what the defense will do and analyze all the other variables at play. It's vital to be prepared on the front end. You create so much muscle memory so that all that stuff is on autopilot. Then you can truly focus on what the defense is doing.

Armed with all that preparation and information, you're better equipped to make big moves on the fly. Your brain is processing things incredibly fast, built on a foundation of hundreds of hours of practice and homework. It can connect points A to B more quickly before you realize what just happened. All that work enables you to deal with storms in life and to make pivots and changes.

You don't know when that big promotion is coming for you. If you're an employee, you don't know when that big break is going to happen. But if you prepare every day, and you keep stacking wins each day, you're going to be ready for that moment in life, just because you're controlling what you can control. It's the best thing you can do because you don't know when that opportunity is coming for you.

Sometimes the Bills were backed up on their two-yard line. That's a tough spot to be in during a game. When you're in that position, the number one goal is to get the first down because then, if you punt, you can get further away from your end zone. But if you don't get that first down, you can't even worry about scoring points. If you don't get that initial first down, the other team's chances of being the next team to score in the game are approximately 90%. So rule number one, when backed into a corner, get a first down.

When you're backed up in a corner in life, quit thinking and take action. Don't think, "I got to go from dead broke to a hundred million." Instead, think about making a slight improvement first. Then, think about your next step and how you can better prepare for the one after that. And so on.

Maybe I took preparation too seriously and still do to this day. But if I didn't have that relentless preparation mentality, I probably never would have made it to the NFL in the first place or even college football. I strive to leave no stone unturned as far as preparation goes. And neither should you.

Because when God puts those opportunities in your life, you want to be completely prepared to run with them.

Key Takeaways

Here are the key takeaways from this chapter:

- The most significant part of success is preparation—the art of controlling the things you can control.
  - Preparing takes intentionality, self-discipline, and willingness to change. In addition, you have to want the long-term goal enough to make those changes.
  - There is no substitute for hard work and preparation.
- Consistency comes with preparation.
  - Focusing on process goals helps you get to your long-term goals.
  - Success is won on a day-to-day basis.
- Be a champion for your high standards of performance.
  - You alone control the effort you put into anything.
  - If you're not going forward in your efforts, you're going backward.
- With great preparation comes great confidence.
  - Preparation enables you to better strategize and improvise in the moment.
  - Preparation better prepares you to handle setbacks and pivot.
  - Sometimes focusing on a small improvement is the best thing you can do to move forward.
  - When God gives you great opportunities in life, you want to be prepared to run with them.

ABOUT THE AUTHOR

After a Hall of Fame career as an All-American at the University of Louisville, Eric Wood was a first-round NFL draft pick by the Buffalo Bills in 2009. He played nine seasons with the Bills, which included a Pro Bowl and two Walter Payton Man of the Year nominations. In 2018, he suffered a career-ending neck injury that has led him on a journey to find out what's next for him.

After calling football games for Fox, ESPN, and CBS early on in his journey, Eric is currently the radio analyst for the Buffalo Bills and the host of the "What's Next with Eric Wood" podcast, where he interviews high achievers in a variety of fields. Eric is a keynote speaker, author, and performance coach who is driven by a passion to help others achieve the best versions of themselves. He uses years of training and coaching from the top minds in his field to promote dedication and hard work at any stage.

Eric is married to his beautiful wife, Leslie, and has two children, Grace and Garrett.

INDEX